2

Summer Flambé'

A Novel

by

Paisley Ray

Text Copyright ©2012 Paisley Ray
Cover Art by Chantal deFelice
Edit by Kristin Lindstrom

ISBN: 1500834319
ISBN-13: 978-1-5008343-1-9
Library of Congress Control Number: TX007628438

The Rachael O'Brien Chronicles
by
Paisley Ray

"A man's kiss is his signature."
~Mae West

Prologue

I began counting the days left in my freshmore break. Sixty-six. I wasn't a freshman anymore—hallelujah! I'd left that journey behind. The fall term hadn't started yet, so I didn't consider myself an official sophomore. Trapped in Canton, Ohio, limbo, away from my friends and potential boyfriend, I held low expectations for my first college summer at home.

Still intact, I considered my virginity to be like an unsightly mole that I needed to lose. But my entrance into womanhood would have to wait until I returned to North Carolina College. It wasn't likely I'd meet anyone lustworthy over the summer.

I was over knockdown dramas and hidden agendas. The best summer I could hope for was a quick one where I encountered as little face time with Dad's girlfriend as possible. I was nineteen, practically a twenty-year-old. I'd come to terms with the fact that my father now dated, but I hadn't warmed to the specimen he'd chosen. She was bound to materialize, and when she did, I planned to lay low and avoid her. My dad and Trudy Bleaux had nothing in common that I could see. The thrill of their tonic's fizz had to be receding, and I was betting that their tryst would go flat before the Fourth of July

1

Stale and Soggy

I needed a distraction, some sort of *flambé* in my SUMMER. Alone in my Canton, Ohio, bedroom the only light came from my lit cigarette. I amused myself by igniting a lone maple leaf that stuck to my windowsill and watched the dark green sear yellow and orange before turning black and ashen. Sucking my cheeks in, I made fish lips in an attempt to blow smoke circles out the window. The stifling night air hung about me like a velvet curtain. A barn owl screeched somewhere outside, and I strained my eyes against the darkness to locate the feathery predator. Ignoring the distant ringing phone, I inhaled deeply and held a tobacco plume in my chest. With summer in front of me, I had loads of free time to learn how to make creative shapes from smoke.

Lately Dad got more calls from Trudy than I did from my girlfriends. That was not right! In defiance, I'd turned off the ringer on my bedroom phone. Contouring my lips, I huffed a controlled breath from my lungs.

The stairs creaked and Dad shouted, "Rachael, it's for you."

I choked while quickly snubbing my cigarette out on the metal window frame channel. Hiding the unfinished evidence in a wooden box that rested on my nightstand, I shouted, "Who is it?"

"Not sure. Someone with a southern accent."

Hoping it was Clay, I unwrapped a wintergreen Certs and placed it on my tongue. Last time I'd seen him, my bra was on the floor of his dorm room and my higher learning was progressing nicely until Agent Storm Cauldwell interrupted our end-of-the-year "study" session. When I'd left his room to give a statement to the FBI, things were awkward. Hoping to get back on the romance track, I mustered up my newly found sultry, picked up the phone, and whispered a sleepy, "Hello."

"Rach, you're never going to believe what's happened to me."

I waited until I heard my father hang up the receiver. "Katie Lee, what's going on?"

"It's Nash, he's left town for the summer."

"Wait a minute, you two broke up. Why do you care?"

She sighed. "I think I drove him away."

"How'd you do that?"

"I was in Big Blue with Gavin Snarks."

"Nice. Have I met him?"

"Maybe at Billy Ray's."

Hearing that name made me cringe. As much as I wanted to forget his thick fingers strangling my neck, I hadn't.

"After store hours we parked Big Blue in the Piggly Wiggly lot and moved into the backseat."

"Did you use protection?"

"We didn't get that far. The windows steamed up. When I cranked 'em down to let air in, I smelled cigarettes. Nash was lurking in the shadows. He'd parked his truck on the street and was leaning against it. He knows Gavin and I were fooling around. The next day I went over to his house to tell him to quit following me around town."

"Why'd you do that?"

"So he'd follow me around town."

"Katie Lee, that's mental."

"I can't help it. I miss him."

"So what exactly is the problem?"

"His mama told me he'd packed up and left. Gone to live with his daddy and work on the oyster farms in Mobile for the summer."

Outside my open window, a car door slammed, and I pried my curtain aside. The moon had set the night landscape aglow in crisp black and white. I watched a woman climb out of a Volkswagen convertible.

"Forget him. Why don't you pay more attention to the guy you had in the backseat of Big Blue?"

"Gavin's good looking, but his personality's as dry as a saltine cracker. When we're together, he never says more than two words, and I do all the talking. He's too much work to be around."

"Why were you with him anyway?"

"I don't want Nash to think I'm still sweet on him."

Even in the dark, I could see a leotard and tights carrying a pillow and an oversized shoulder bag. "Damn."

"Exactly," Katie Lee said.

The doorbell rang, and instinctively I knew I was about to ingest a higher-than-recommended dose of Dad's girlfriend, Trudy Bleaux.

"Katie Lee, I gotta go. Trudy just rang the doorbell. She's carrying an overnight bag. This can't be good."

"Oh Lord. Call me back when she's gone."

DAD HAD A SECRET and kept it hidden. Even though he's a staunch Cleveland Browns football fan, his favorite beer is made in their biggest rival's hometown. Dad drinks Iron City Beer, brewed and canned in Pittsburgh. I'd been in relax mode until Trudy's high-octane rasp rattled my inner ear. She had missed kindergarten 101 and didn't remember to keep a quiet indoor voice. She used an all-purpose, perkified frequency range, which I imagined she amped up when she taught her aerobic classes.

For Dad's sake, I'd promised myself to tolerate her and mind my own business. That task was easier when I was at school, separated from her by two states. I snuck down the stairs and turned a corner toward the garage to snatch a cold one from the fridge. I guzzled a quarter of the can to dull my sensitivity to her presence. Careful not to let the door into the house slam, I scurried halfway up the stairs and ducked behind the half wall where the railing ended.

I'd never witnessed Trudy's evening look. Whenever I saw her, it was in passing, and I mostly wished she'd disappear. She didn't have her makeup mask on, and a butterfly wing constellation of freckles splattered her cheeks. Her hair had been styled with a mixer. Not the dough or batter attachment, but the wire one for blending dry ingredients. She'd woven her hair in and out of the spaces between the beater blades.

"Trudy," Dad said. "It's near midnight."

"John," she blurted. "Someone broke into my apartment. Have you been reading the newspaper? There's been a rash of home robberies, and I've been victimized."

Dad wrapped his arm around her shoulders and guided her to the sofa. "Are you hurt?"

"No, I'm not hurt."

"Tell me what happened."

She grabbed a crumpled tissue from an outside pocket in her gym bag and blew her nose. "I taught the nine o'clock step class. Afterward I showered and changed at the gym. I needed flax seed, sardines, and spinach for my morning smoothie, so I went to the Valu-King. When I got home, I unlocked my door, and my apartment was—all tidied up."

Leaning forward, I peered at the two through the wood railing slats. They were oblivious to my presence. What a cockamamie story. Of all the bullshit things to say. Dad was not going to fall for this. It was the most asinine reason for throwing yourself at someone that I'd ever heard.

Dad tipped his head. "Tidied up?"

"You know. Cleaned, organized."

"I'm not sure I understand."

"You've seen my apartment. I live eclectically. I don't believe that kitchen utensils should be confined to drawers, and I like to style my hair and makeup by the entry closet."

I thought about interrupting to ask if she used the kitchen sink instead of the toilet, but refrained.

"Someone," she sniffled, "violated my apartment. Kitchen stuff is in the kitchen, and bathroom stuff is in the bathroom. Throws were folded, mirrors moved—you can see the furniture—and my bed's been made. My apartment smells like Windex."

Dad rubbed Trudy's shoulder, which made me want to hurl. These two were so opposite they couldn't possibly last. I told myself he was just rebelling against Mom's abrupt departure. Inside my head, I chanted the mantra, "Trudy's just a phase."

"I'm sure there's an explanation. Someone thought they were doing you a favor."

"Who would do that? I can't find a thing."

"Maybe Sky stopped by."

Trudy scoffed. "She'd never clean my apartment. She knows better."

"Give her a call. At least you'll know if it was your sister's doing."

Trudy puffed an anxious breath and turned her puppy eyes on my father. "I guess I could call her in the morning, but can I stay here tonight?"

Clearing my throat, I walked down the stairs. "What's going on?"

NOTE TO SELF
Katie Lee and Nash finally spending some quality time apart. Hoping it lasts so sophomore year will be drama free.

Trudy is weaseling her way into our house. Must come up with diversionary tactic.

Trudy has a sister, Sky Bleaux. Figures.

2

Bad Energy

Dad was an early riser, and by default so was I. Trudy was not. Every morning before I left for the restoration shop, I warmed an icing-coated strawberry Pop Tart in the toaster. Working at the family art restoration business had pros and cons. On the plus side, I could wear whatever. On the negative, I carpooled with Dad, spending more hours in a confined space with a PU—parental unit—than recommended by a recent poll in *Seventeen* magazine. Luckily he and I didn't delve into any overly personal conversations. Mostly we focused on work.

In late June, someone flicked a circuit breaker, and the heat index soared to sweltering hot. Being sweaty in a house without central air-conditioning, and confined in close quarters with Dad's girlfriend, brings on irritability. I needed to convince Dad of two things: first, to install central A/C—admittedly dicey since our house is a fifty-year-old antique—and second, to ditch his Trudy habit.

To ease her visitor-imposition conscience, Dad's girlfriend initiated annoying acts of helpfulness. She'd step aside when I met her in the hallway, and in the evening, she patted the sofa with her hand in an attempt to lure me into the prime TV viewing seat. She preached the benefits of folic acid, fiber, and a slew of vitamins whenever I ate something from a box. She said she needed a new sports bra and wanted me to go to the mall with her. *Yeah, right.*

She was a master irritator, and by week two her overexercised, bounce-a-penny ass that still slept on our sofa grated under my skin. Leaving the kitchen table set for a cereal breakfast for me and washing a load of my laundry triggered menacing thoughts toward her well-being. I'd met an abundance of fakers my freshman year at college. Having experience with deviant unstable types, I determined her nicey-nice façade had to be a ruse. She wasn't right for Dad. He couldn't possibly be happy with her. She was just the first thing that came along since Mom left. Unselfishly, I decided to take it upon myself to crack her sunshiny shell.

Step one, surveillance. I kept a close eye on her and interrupted any potential lovey-dovey PDA—public displays of affection—she initiated toward Dad. I became a regular *Late Night with David Letterman* viewer and slept with my bedroom light on to give the illusion that I was still awake. I hoped this ploy would curtail after-dark alone-time between the two. The mere thought of her eggbeaters on Mom's side of the bed harmed my sanity. Step two, extermination. The sooner Trudy moved her jumping-jacked glutes back to her apartment, the less professional time I'd need to restore my mental health.

THE GRAVEL IN THE driveway outside Dad's shop crunched beneath his feet, drowning any early morning nature noises. I'd stayed up late the night before talking on the phone with Katie Lee and secretly smoking cigarettes. The conversation was one-sided. She wallowed over Nash, and I listened. It was no use trying to talk sense into my roommate. I knew better. Occasionally I interjected questions for her to ponder. "If he were behind bars, would you still want a relationship?

Don't you think there is more than one person out there who you could be crazy-attracted to?"

She rebutted my second question. "You tell me. Is there another Clay out there? Or is he the only one?"

I hated when she did that. *Smartass.*

My father was a walking history book and rattled on about seventeenth-century ripple-molded frames in polished hardwoods. He appreciated repairing the pieces that had traveled through time. His size eleven feet stomped quickly up to the building. "We received a commission from the Canton Museum to refurbish twenty picture frames. Touching up stain and gold leaf, making sure the molding is intact. I said we'd have them completed in a week. I can really use your help."

After disarming the alarm, he headed for the coffee maker. I looked at him suspiciously.

"What?" he asked.

"Nothing," I said.

We both knew that Trudy preached the ill effects of caffeinated drinks. While the coffee pot finished percolating, he and I slid on our aprons and surgical gloves. He laid two of the frames on the worktable and pointed out where time, humidity, and mishandling had cracked the wood and damaged the carvings. As he and I worked, my mind morphed on the intricacies of the task, sweeping me away from time and place. He showed me how to apply an epoxy on chipped carvings, adjusting viscosity so it didn't ooze and dry in globs. Once we finished, we'd have to wait for the chemical bond to dry.

Dad pointed to a pair of Louis XIV armchairs. "Think you're up for repairing them?"

I gave him a nod-shrug. Moving toward the chairs, I admired the ornately carved frame. When I started a new project, I found myself wondering how many homes the piece had lived in. My fingers brushed over the curves of the arms. I guessed these hadn't been look-see antiques, chosen to be displayed as a tribute to acquired or pretend wealth. These had been owned by someone who didn't know what they had or didn't give a rip.

Dings and chips around the legs had been delivered like a round of ammunition that lodged precise and deep. I imagined a child, unfairly disciplined, releasing frustration with a steady kick on the supple wood, while administering a sharp fingernail or the edge of a toy on the arm carvings. It would take a lot of work to make these look new, and I didn't know if I could piece the carvings back together without making it look amateur.

I fumbled with a corner square of sandpaper, and Dad interrupted me. He unrolled a felt case and offered me his woodworking tools. Dancing my fingers over the worn-handled chisels, I scanned the variances in shape and size of blades. I removed my favorite tool from his case. It looked like a paintbrush, except the tip held a piece of sandpaper no bigger than your thumb. I used it to smooth scrollwork and hard-to-get-at corners.

Dad smiled. "That's one of a kind, designed by your grandfather."

We used an array of stains and paints, but Dad recommended I use potassium dichromate. Toxic stuff—orange and red crystals that came in a tin. He taught me how to mix the right consistency and color. We tested it on a piece of scrap mahogany and watched it react with the tannins, producing a rich brown stain. Later on, Edmond, Dad's longtime assistant, would show me how to reupholster the seat.

Once I'd finished gluing loose joints on two chair legs, I plugged in a fan to speed up the drying. My stomach gurgled, and the bell on the door chimed.

Looking up, I did a double take. Dad had ordered takeout lunch, and I knew the delivery guy. Markus Doneski had gone to high school with me. While Dad went to get money, Markus moved toward me and muttered, "Well, well. If it ain't Arty Farty O'Brien."

I hadn't seen Doneski in a year and had actually fed his memory into my brain shredder. "Markus," I scowled.

"Miss me?" he asked.

"Ah, let me think. NO."

Dad returned from the office. "You two know each other?"

"Of course. I sat behind Rachael in trigonometry."

Dad handed him a twenty. "Oh, nice. I bet you two have some catch-ing up."

I seared Markus with my eyes. I wouldn't be ordering anything from the Hoagie House anytime soon.

THE CANTON MUSEUM OF ART had a new exhibit, and my dad went over to help the curator, who was also a close friend of his. Figuring the chairs needed time to dry, and since the phone was not ringing off the hook, I took a leisurely lunch out back. After I ate my Italian hoagie, I closed my eyes and worked on maintaining my daily dose of sun-induced vitamin D.

Dad's assistant, Edmond, didn't hear me come back from lunch. Climbing onto a stool, I half watched him shimmy his hips in a dance around a worktable. He sang with Elvis about being all shook up. Swiveling his pointer fingers toward me, he softened the volume. His forehead looked moist. In a winded breath, he sputtered, "There you are."

I walked over and dabbed his forehead with a rag. "Is this what you do when you're"—I looked behind each of my shoulders—"alone?"

He chuckled, and his cheeks reddened, softening his badass biker look. His shoulder-length black hair had grayed near his face, and he pulled it all back in a ponytail. The denim shirt and jeans he wore, combined with his furniture-polish-stained hands, fit the mold of a grease monkey, not a sophisticated restoration expert. "You make a great spy. Sneaking up on people." He took the rag from my hand and hucked it in the wastebasket. "I don't reveal secrets that easily."

Lunch had landed hard. I rubbed my stomach. "Are there any Tums tablets around?"

"Check the Kittinger drawer," he said.

Stacks of client files and invoices rested on top of an antique walnut desk Dad had rescued. I sat down and dug in the center drawer. I didn't find Tums, but I did find a peppermint Lifesaver. I popped it in my mouth and leafed through the folders. For insurance purposes, Dad always took before, during, and after photos of commissions. The

Canton Museum was a regular client, and files were labeled by department. Some private collectors' invoices also littered the desktop. Dad
must have been working on billing before he left.

I was surprised to see a folder labeled *McCarty*. We did work for
her, which was weird since she and Dad were icy. Geneva McCarty was
a brazen eccentric whom I'd met a handful of times over the years.
I flipped open her folder and leafed through some of the projects.
Judging from the commissions we'd gotten, she had deep pockets.
Mostly furniture repairs for nicks and scratches, gobs of painting
restorations, some custom frames, a velvet jewelry box lining, and
bookbinding. A Polaroid photo of a tattered, leather-bound book
rested in the folder. I picked it up and looked at it closely. A string,
wrapped in a figure eight securing two leather circles, held it closed.
The title was engraved in gold lettering, the first letter of each word
narrow and enlarged, the rest of the letters simple, not ornate. The
book was old, fifteenth or sixteenth century, I guessed. *Nostradamus's
Translation of Horapollon of Manouthis*. A French book of notes on Egyptian
hieroglyphics. Funky. Jogging my memory, I swore I'd seen this book
somewhere.

"Edmond, do you know how to bind books?"

"No, but your father does."

The date on the yellowed invoice was May 1968, the year I was born.
Leaving the desk, I checked on the chair leg glue. "What do you think?"

He tapped the joints with a finger. "Let it dry overnight. Start the
arms in the morning." He motioned with his head. "Give me a hand with
the Tiffany chandelier?"

Sheets of glass and a box of pendants were spread out on a worktable.
Edmond had suspended the lotus flower chandelier on a pulley. Shades of
green ranging from emerald to mint gave the glass the illusion of tangled
vines. Interspersed among the grassy-toned hues were delicate clusters of
soft pinks. He and I traced cardboard templates for the missing glass and
began cutting and grinding replicas. Once we finished, we'd apply copper
foil and weld the pieces into place with a soldering gun.

A luster of light gleamed inside a coin-sized piece of leaded glass Edmond was inspecting. "How are things?"

I smirked. "That's a nonquestion question."

"Things in your life. I like knowing what you're up to, your plans."

"My plan is to work here for college cash and manage to survive summer without becoming mentally scarred by Dad's overzealous space cadet girlfriend." *There, I'd said it.*

Edmond smiled empathetically but didn't make a big deal of my Trudy Bleaux adjective outburst. He was like family, and I allowed him to pry into my personal business. He answered my questions on subjects that I didn't feel comfortable asking Mom or Dad. Topics like my paternal grandparents, who had died before I could walk. Dad went all ice cube when I'd asked about his mother's favorite color and if her handwriting was loopy or chicken scratch. Mom always pleaded the fifth, saying she didn't know. Edmond told me yellow and that her handwriting was like calligraphy, full of twirls and loops. Twenty years older than Dad, he'd worked for my grandparents when he was my age, and he was the only source of information I had about my ancestry.

When Dad inherited the furniture repair business, Edmond encouraged an expansion into fine art. Despite Edmond's need to know my business, I categorized him under favorite, most trusted family friend.

I traced a template for a missing piece of glass in the Tiffany.

"Life doesn't stand still. Whether we like it or not, it fluxes."

The battered chandelier we worked on was testament to that nugget of wisdom. "Who brought in the..."

He turned on the grinder, drowning my words. I watched him smooth a piece of glass. Repairing the chandelier was like fitting a jigsaw puzzle, and I didn't look at the clock until the light streaming through the windows faded.

Removing his protective glasses, Edmond wiped the lenses.

I looked at the Swatch on my wrist. "Why hasn't Dad called?"

"He must be held up in traffic."

We tidied up the worktable, and Edmond turned off the lights. He wheeled his twelve-speed Schwinn Le Tour limited edition outside and set the alarm on the shop before he locked the door. The two of us sat in the mahogany Adirondack chairs, a barter trade from an artisan, that rested on a cement slab patio outside the shop.

He patted my knee. "I'll stick around. Make sure he shows."

A smoky haze of low clouds drifted across the sky, diffusing the sunlight. It was perfect weather for shorts, t-shirts, no shoes. At least for a few hours until the mosquitoes began to feast.

Chin up, he rested his closed eyes.

Watching the road for Dad, I asked, "Big weekend plans?"

"Planting snap peas and beets."

He had been on the planet three times longer than I had, but defied age. His brown eyes were bright; his skin had some roadways, but no potholes or loose guide rails. His picket teeth gleamed of youth. In junior high, I'd asked him his secret. He told me: eat colorful vegetables, run like you're being chased, Albolene cream on your face, elbows, and feet every night, and brush your teeth with baking soda.

Tilting his head forward, he asked, "What about you? Any plans?"

"Just hanging out. Hoping Trudy reclutters her apartment and deems it habitable. My opinion of her would move up a notch if she moved back to her own space this weekend."

Adjusting his graying ponytail, he suppressed a smile. "You don't approve of Trudy?"

Edmond was a perceptive guy. I grimaced, wondering why he'd bothered to ask. Then again, unlike Dad, he'd asked. "She's okay at a distance."

A horn beeped from a two-door marigold Volkswagen Cabriolet convertible. The top was down. Nothing about Trudy was ordinary, and even her curls defiantly cascaded out of the silk scarf she'd fastened over her head. Black-and-white-checkered-frame sunglasses, scattered with neon shapes, edged down her nose. She could lose the head gear, but the car she drove was killer. I'd never tell her, but I drooled over her transportation.

Pebbles crunched beneath the tires. There was a female passenger in the front seat. Despite different hair color and cuts, the two women had strikingly similar walnut-colored eyes and delicate noses that narrowed on the edge. Trudy put the car in park and waved over enthusiastically. "Hi, Rachael, hi, Edmond."

"Trudy, how are you doing?" Edmond asked.

I didn't say anything, figuring not much had changed since I'd seen her eight hours ago.

She slammed her door and sprang toward us. "I am fab-u-lous-so."

Edmond slipped on his helmet.

Squeezing his bicep, she said, "Glad to see you've been working out."

Color rose in his cheeks. "Just pedaling."

"Where's Dad?" I asked, secretly fantasizing she'd dump him for a more mature Edmond and his shapely biceps.

Trudy adjusted her sunglasses and placed her hands on her hips. Sucking wind, she let out a sigh that flushed a crow out of a nearby buckeye tree. "John was held up at the museum." She smiled. "He asked me to pick you up. He'll meet us back at the house."

Why didn't Dad have the decency to call and tell me himself? That pissed me off. Trudy was not someone I wanted to spend any additional time with, not to mention the girl in her car whose arms hung over the passenger door. Her jet-black dyed hair draped down her shoulders, and she futzed with an orange chunk that hung in her eyes. She began lacing it around her slim index finger while she cracked gum in a round of snaps. "Rachael, Edmond, this is my sister, Sky."

Sky popped her head up and smiled. Instead of waving, she separated her fingers down the middle, and saluted us a la Spock. She looked to be in her early twenties, well past the age of pretend. "Trudy, we need to get going. I have to prepare notes for the MUFON meeting tonight."

"MUFON?" I asked.

Sky sat up. "Mutual UFO Network. If you're not doing anything, come to our midnight meeting. We're looking for new members. I could pick you up after my shift at Orange Julius juice bar."

Two with the same gene pool. Great. "I have plans," I mumbled as I clambered into the back seat of Trudy's convertible.

Dad and I needed to have a chat. Trudy was not my buddy, and I was not cool with being chauffeured by her. I needed my own wheels. Four of them.

LIKE A FUDGE POP on a stick, my fingertips were stained brown, and the edges of my nails had split. I peeled back the flappy bits that looked vulnerable to being snagged.

"Power Boost," Trudy said, "is an easy source of globular isolated proteins. Make sure you mention that when you sell the powder."

On the car ride to the house, I gathered that Trudy and Sky had signed on to sell some energy powder.

Sky pulled out a map of Canton. Strategizing a door-to-door blitz that would rival any Avon representation, she'd highlighted some sections in pink and others in yellow. "You take the east neighborhoods, and I'll take the west," she told Trudy.

At a stoplight, Trudy twisted her head back toward me. "Rachael, are you interested in making some extra cash?"

Contorting the corners of my eyes and mouth downward, I flashed a *yeah, right* nonverbal response. I had experience drinking concoctions and had ended up shagging a three-step with a creep who later tried to throttle me. And then there was an incident at a clambake where I blacked out. I now erred on the cautious side when it came to consuming offered liquids. Peddling protein powder to unsuspecting Cantonians would be a nonhappening event.

Trudy had good traffic light karma. Riding in her open-top car was the beauty salon equivalent of having my hair styled in a wind tunnel. By the time she parked in front of my house, my ponytail had been twirled into a complicated web of tangles and insects. Sidling out of the backseat, I self-consciously rubbed a hand across a cluster of flyaway hair. Luckily the only person around was a kid who struggled with a dodgy pull cord on a push lawn mower.

Trudy readjusted her headscarf, retying it around her forehead. Jovially she chattered an unhelpful observation. "Rachael, your left calf doesn't have the same muscle tone as your right."

Pulling a stack of mail from the metal box, I twisted to look at the backs of my legs. I hadn't told Trudy about the night Big Blue, my college roommate's Oldsmobile, had been purposely driven over me by a frenemy.

I leafed through junk mail while Trudy unloaded cans of Energy Boost from a case in the trunk of her car. She lectured, "Daily protein powder and my step class will build strength and have you toned by the end of summer."

Sky slammed the car door, then folded her body in half in a touch-the-toe stretch before moving to help Trudy sort and divide the cans. "I'll sell at least a dozen at MUFON tonight," she said.

Flipping through the magazines and bills a second time, I hoped for a letter from Clay. Our last parting had been abrupt, and we'd left our relationship open-ended. I wasn't even sure if he'd speak to me when I returned to campus. I'd mulled over the details of our lip-lock in his dorm room and shared the series of events with Katie Lee. We both agreed that I couldn't have stopped the interruption, i.e., Storm Cauldwell from the FBI showing up unannounced as Clay and I explored...things.

Bent down beside me, Sky plucked a dandelion cluster out of a sidewalk seam and ate it. "Expecting something important?"

I fastened the metal door on the mailbox and grimaced. "Some dog could've marinated that."

"Yum," she smiled.

Trudy closed the roof on her convertible. "Dandelion leaves are a body tonic. They provide more vitamin A than carrots and support your liver..."

In defeat, I left the two on the street and marched up to my house. As I inserted a key to unlock the dead bolt, the front door opened without effort. Pot roast heaven wafted in my face. The kind smothered in onion and garlic gravy, with sweet baby carrots, celery hearts, finger potatoes, and garden tomatoes—just like Mom used to make.

My back stiffened. Dad only cooked cereal and toast. I dropped the mail in the entry and tiptoed toward the kitchen, careful to avoid the loose hallway floorboard.

Soapy water filled half of the sink. Spices were out of the drawer and aligned next to the oven. Steam rose from two bread loaves resting on the cutting board. She was seated, her shoulders pulling the back of her sleeveless blouse seams taught. Her tanned arms were solider than I re-membered. When I looked at the back of her head, I wasn't sure. Her hair was shoulder length with a touch of gray. Across from her a woman with short white hair, shaved in the back and spiked on top, looked up at me.

"Mom?"

NOTE TO SELF
I am not okay carpooling with Trudy. How am I going to convince Dad to get me a car?

Mom's back, and she's still hanging with Betts, the head nut-case she ran off with. Shit!

3

In the Cards

She turned before rising from the chair. My eyes lingered above her smile, on the shadows that darkened the skin beneath her eyes. Hesitantly she said, "Rachael."

I fell into her open arms. "Why didn't anyone tell me you were coming?"

Before she answered, Dad walked in the back door and froze. "Maeve? What are you...? How did you get in?"

Mom brushed imaginary creases off her pants. "The house was unlocked."

Dad glared at me as if I'd let them in the house. Staring back, I shrugged. Wheels inside his head seemed to grind, until an epiphany stuck, and he remembered his girlfriend had been the last to leave. He pinched his lips when Trudy stepped into the kitchen, scarf tails dangling behind her shoulder. Her head swiveled like a bobble from Mom to Dad. In the doorway, Sky stood on tiptoes and peered over her sister's shoulder. "Hello."

Mom moved toward them. "Maeve O'Brien. I don't believe we've met."

Trudy gave a curious stare. My mom's arrival was as welcome as a turd in a punch bowl.

Six people standing around a farmhouse kitchen was like being in a nylon tent at Girl Scout camp, and I moved toward the screen door for airflow.

"Rachael, aren't you going to introduce your friends?" Mom asked. "Please stay for dinner. There's plenty."

"Dinner? Maeve, you can't just show up and expect us to—eat."

I was miffed that she invited Dad's girlfriend and her sister to stay, but figured they wouldn't. They'd get it. *I was wrong.*

Trudy clasped her hands together and said, "I've heard so much about you. I mean, um, er—" her words bumbled in nonsense.

"Well yes, lovely to meet you. Were all you girls in high school together?"

Dad cringed and Sky snorted. I didn't know Trudy's precise age. It was somewhere between too young to be my mother and too old to be my sister. I guessed I wasn't the only one who wished there was an open bottle of something alcoholic nearby.

Mom hadn't processed that this was Dad's girlfriend until he told her. "Maeve, this is my friend, Trudy."

God, it was hot in the kitchen.

"And her sister, Sky."

An uncensored wince took hold of Mom.

Her friend reached an arm around her. "Hi, everyone, I'm Betts, Maeve's friend."

The air was clear. They both had friends.

Great, Mom was traveling with her head nut-o, which probably meant she hadn't returned to woo herself back into Dad's arms and my good graces.

Offering to shake Trudy's hand, Betts flipped it over and traced her palm. Upon release, Betts stepped back and made a show of rotating her head as if encircling Trudy from head to toe, which I thought brave. I normally took the opposite approach and tried not to look below Trudy's neck where she glowed in a lightning-bug-colored thongtard over bumblebee leggings. "Aquarius," Betts said, hanging on the *s* like a serpent.

Trudy rubbed the hairs on her left arm. "How did you know?"

"It's in your aura. Purple. You are visionary and inventive."

Dad scoffed, and I smirked. Betts had a creative way of complimenting Trudy.

The kitchen went awkward silent as eyeballs darted around the room. "Maeve," Dad said. "You can't just show up and expect us to eat pot roast."

Mom started opening drawers, pulling out serving utensils. "I know we have things to discuss, but that can wait." Her eyes lingered on me. "It would be a shame to waste the roast." Moving past me, she opened the screen door, "Rachael, can you carry the bread?"

"No, she can't carry the bread. You can't just walk back into our lives like you never left." Dad kicked the metal garbage can, knocking it over and rolling it into the butcher-block island.

The sweet and savory smells sent me into my file cabinet of memories. Not a specific event, but more of a slide show of the seasons of my childhood. I looked at Dad, waiting for his lead, wondering if he'd chuck the roast and Mom out of the house. He threw his hands up and pressed them into his scalp.

"The pot roast does smell amazing," I said.

Mom rubbed her hand across my back.

Exasperated, Dad gestured to the back door. "It's too hot to eat inside."

Setting the picnic table and carrying food and drinks outside stifled the awkwardness that had settled inside the house. After a second helping of baby carrots smothered in gravy, I pushed my paper plate aside. Darkness began to swallow the last flicker of dusk. Mom's unannounced visit confused more than enraged me. Since she'd left, time had snuffed out the embers under Dad's and my emotional cauldrons, but her return was the spark that slowly brought wounded feelings bubbling back up.

Backyard floodlights baited a growing congregation of winged insects, and they fluttered under the warm white glow. I waited for Trudy and Sky to peddle the protein powder to Mom and her psychic leader. They didn't mention it, but the night wasn't over.

Plastering a toothy smile on her face that stuck as she chewed, Trudy took advantage of the crammed wood bench. Merging her left side into Dad's right, they molded together like two colors of Play-Doh squeezed through a dough press.

Sky carried the dinner conversation, firing questions about parapsychological phenomena, which I found out is the umbrella for haunting, out-of-body and near-death experiences, clairvoyance, and reincarnation. The topic sent Dad's brow into a crinkle, and I guessed he wished he could transport himself somewhere far away.

Betts, not Mom, answered Sky's questions with nondefinitive statements. "Meditation and levitation," she said, "are about tuning into one's spiritual energy. Maeve's progressing. Just last night under the trees before sunset, she had a breakthrough and reached a higher plateau of consciousness."

Betts's red aura blinked on my radar.

Dad asked, "Where are you two staying?"

"At a campsite near Lake O' Pines," Mom said.

His mouth gaped. "You have to be kidding. You're staying in a tent? Without running water or a shower?"

Mom's eyes turned down.

"God, Maeve, is that what you want? To live like a gypsy?"

"Maeve and I prefer a more simple existence. We don't require all the materialism in our lives."

Dad held his hand up. "Just stop. You two can stay in the apartment above the shop."

"John, that's kind of you, but—"

"I insist," he said, slipping Mom the key from his ring.

Mom thanked Dad.

Sky looked up into the night, and asked Betts, "What's your sign?"

Betts followed Sky's heavenward gaze. "What an insightful question. There is a correlation between the planets and horoscopes."

My eyes lingered on the gelled spikes in Betts's hair. They grew out of her scalp like a forest of toothpicks. How had she enticed my mother to run off to Sedona? Was it a change in lifestyle that Mom craved, or the thrill of an adventure she couldn't fulfill living in Ohio with Dad and me? Had Mom gone lesbian? I didn't want to go there, but couldn't squelch the question. Betts's towering, thick-boned shell looked androgynous-ish. She softened it with billowy clothes, dangly bracelets, and rings on her thumbs.

The thought of Mom "romantically" liking a woman twisted a nervous-sickish feeling in my stomach. She and Dad weren't into public displays of affection, which would be gross. No one wants to see their PUs—parental units—making out. I'd always merged them into one parental team: working at the shop, keeping the day-to-day going, falling asleep on the sofa in the evening. Had Mom been that conflicted sexually and run away so she could let loose with Betts?

Sky poked a carrot and asked, "Do you levitate?"

"As I mentioned, levitation can only be attained during high levels of consciousness. I work toward clarity and mystical rapture."

"Have you read that collection of prophecies by that French dude?" Sky asked.

Mom sipped her wine. "You mean Nostredame?"

"Yeah, him. He wrote a book in like the fifteen hundreds. Predicted wars, earthquakes, natural disasters."

Patting Betts on the shoulder, Mom said, "Betts is a follower of Nostradamus. She's fluent in French and Latin, and spent years studying spiritualism outside Lyon."

Betts waved Mom's bragging aside.

I found myself paying more attention to my mother's movements than to her words. How did she react to Betts? Did her hand linger? Dad had been right. Pot roast was a crummy idea. Now it felt like a brick in my stomach, distracting me from sorting out my head. Initial joy had surged at seeing Mom in person, but now my emotions were unraveling, and I felt a loss thinking that the mom who sat across from me might not be the person that I thought I'd wanted back. Outwardly, she worked to appear carefree, though I wondered if she slept soundly, or did something inside her knot, giving her fitful nights that created the circles under her eyes.

"We've studied Nostradamus in group," Mom said.

"What museum houses his manuscript?" I asked.

Gulping from a highball glass, Betts clunked it onto the patio table. She'd produced her own whisky bottle when everyone else opted for wine. She had a peculiar habit of clearing her throat with a thwarty grunt when she emptied her glass.

"The book isn't in a museum," Dad said.

"Where is it?" Sky asked.

Betts toyed with the ruby cabochon stone set in her antique thumb ring. "It's been debated for centuries as to whether or not there is a missing fifteen sixty-six edition of the prophecies." Her eyes twinkled, and she downed her whisky to the bottom. "It would be a priceless artifact to have in a collection."

Trudy forgot how to speak in sentences and replied with nervous single syllable grunts of recognition, wary of the two self-professed psychics, as though they were capable of altering her fortune.

"Are you a collector?" I asked.

Dad hadn't eaten Mom's pot roast, only poked it around his plate. For the first time all night, he looked at Betts with curiosity.

"Anyone for dessert?" Mom asked as she stood to move inside. "Cherries jubilee."

Topping up her glass, Betts said, "I travel under the guidance of the stars. The only thing I collect is knowledge."

Bile rose in my throat at her empty meringue rhetoric. The bullshit washed fatigue into my shoulders. I didn't know my mom, and probably never had.

The back screen clanked. Kitchen gadgetry was Mom's weakness, and it looked as though there was one thing about her that hadn't changed. She held a pie plate in one hand and a blowtorch in the other.

Sky slid off the bench and helped Mom with dessert. She pointed to the pyro device and asked, "What's that for?"

"Do you know what you're doing?" Dad asked.

Mom turned on the torch. It made a noise like the spit sucker they put in your mouth at the dentist. "Burns off the cognac and puts a warm crust on the top shell of the jubilee."

As Betts took a hefty swig from her glass, I locked my eyes into hers and raised my voice. "Are you and my mom involved—sexually?" I looked at Mom. "Is that why you left?"

The table went quiet, and only the neighbor's pool pump kicking on provided background noise. No one moved, unless you count Dad's jaw dropping and Betts choking on her shot.

"Rachael," Mom blurted out, just as Betts hosed a spray of whisky. Forgetting to point her lit torch at dessert, the two connected, arching a flame from Betts's face to the napkin that rested in front of Trudy.

Dad threw Trudy's mint water on the flames that charred the plastic red-and-white-check tablecloth. We all jumped out of the picnic benches, and Dad ran for a fire extinguisher.

Trudy assessed the front of her leotard. Splatters of flaming whisky had made contact with the spandex and bored a series of random holes in the fabric.

Returning at a sprint with an extinguisher, Dad fumbled with the safety catch. "Stand back, everyone."

I glared at Betts. She dabbed the corners of her mouth and under her nose. "Your mother and I were born under complementary planets. We see our future pursuits with clarity and do not muddy the divine calling with fleeting desires."

"I'm confused," Sky said. "Does that mean you are or aren't lesbos?"

Tossing the safety pin aside, Dad fired the extinguisher, sending clouds of white fog over the flaming table.

"Oh, the dessert," Mom complained.

I wasn't in the mood for anything named jubilee.

Deflating his shoulders, Dad clipped, "You left me to be with a woman?"

Mom's eyes analyzed invisible lint on her lap.

A sheath of foam covered the dirty place settings and Mom's homemade dessert. Turning on his heel, Dad strode toward the garage. Trudy scurried behind him, and Mom trailed along, mumbling something about sleeping arrangements.

After the outdoor-flame-show-gone-amuck, I cleared the melted plastic tablecloth, paper plates, and silverware into the trash. Betts dug in her purse and pulled out a pack of tarot cards. "Would you like a reading?" she asked.

"I don't believe in fortune telling."

"Come on, Rachael," Sky said. "Just for fun."

I stood while Betts laid out a five-card spread. Delivering her spiel, she said, "These represent your present position, present desire, the unexpected, the immediate future, and its outcome."

Was this how you lured my mother? If she could actually see the future, I wondered if she'd tell me when Mom would tire of her company and move back to Canton.

"The magician," she said. "You have an extraordinary memory. A talent you're not using at full potential."

I scowled. Mom must have told her about my photographic memory.

She flipped over another card and spoke from across the table as I tried to look disinterested.

"The high priestess." Betts traced the corners of the card with her finger and lowered her voice.

Sky leaned in to listen.

"You think you want a neat and orderly life. With time, you'll realize that you can't resist untangling confusion, creating order. Righting a wrong." She looked up. "It's your gift."

Wide-eyed, Sky glanced at me but kept her thoughts to herself.

"The chariot. An emotional battle will ensue."

A mosquito landed on my leg, and I killed it. Before I opened the screen door, I asked, "Why are you in town anyway?"

"There's a psychic expo at the convention center. Maeve and I have a booth."

I knew it. Mom wasn't here to see Dad and me. She had an agenda. I watched Mom wander back to the table, apparently having given up on talking to Dad.

Sky stroked her chin. "How many people visit a psychic convention?"

"Thousands," Betts said. "I met the most interesting young man. He's an entrepreneur, sells herbal remedies at a booth near ours." She turned toward the house and spoke loudly. "Maeve and I told him all about you attending North Carolina College. He said he knew some people from that area."

I replied equally as loudly, "North Carolina is a big place. The chances of my knowing him are, like, zil."

"Do you need any help in the booth?" Sky asked. "I could drum up business, talk to customers, and help peddle what you sell."

Drawn back by the conversation, I asked, "How long are you and Mom in town?"

"Until the beginning of August." She flipped two more tarot cards.

"The tower and the lover's card," Mom said.

"Does that mean Rachael will find love in a high-rise?" Sky asked.

Betts smiled. "Rachael attracts complication."

Stepping behind Betts, I looked at the card. In a huff, I gathered the salt and pepper shakers and took them inside. My focus became lost in the spice drawer somewhere between cumin and paprika. *Attracts complication. Like all this was my fault.* I gritted my teeth. Betts was a professional head-gamer, trying to pin the family dysfunction on me.

The screen door opened, startling me. Taking some glasses from Sky's hand, I said, "Thanks."

"Your mom showing up is kind of funky. I think my sister is going to have a heart attack. She doesn't look so good."

I'd warmed to Sky since we'd shared the moment of clarifying that my mom had a female lover. Although Mom hadn't willingly professed their relationship, it seemed obvious. Reaching into the liquor cabinet, I pulled out crème de menthe. "Want some?"

Sky found two coffee mugs while I popped cubes out of the freezer trays.

"Can we talk?" she whispered.

After pouring the green liquid over ice, I tucked the bottle away.

Stepping out of earshot from the screen door, she said, "Your dad seems nice enough, but he's too old for my sister. Your mom showing up complicates things. It'll force Trudy to think about finding someone her own age without baggage."

Sky Bleaux's words were the most sensible enlightenment I'd heard all evening, but I wondered, *what was the baggage she'd referred to?*

Clinking her glass to mine, she made a toast. "Here's to helping the stars between Trudy and your dad combust." After taking a sip, she smiled with green-stained teeth.

I downed my after-dinner cordial. "I'm in."

OUR NINETEEN THIRTY FARMHOUSE had original plaster walls, wood floors, and ditsy floral wallpaper in the hallway. Mom and Dad had foregone installing central air-conditioning. It was charming, except in summer. A second-floor electric ceiling fan hummed as it battled the summer heat. Like the spinning blades cutting hot air, I wrestled with the insanity of my family mechanics. Corpselike I lay motionless on my bed, somehow hoping to squelch the fact that both Dad and Mom had girlfriends. The light bulb that glowed on my bed-side table added a wave of heat to the warm air that coursed over my lethargic body. My brain had short-circuited, and an ache pinged in my head. I couldn't sleep.

I turned off the lamp, lit a cigarette, and dialed Travis's number. He had a knack for perspective, could massage my insecurities, and offered sound advice. Besides professing his gaydom to me when I had made a pass at him in his dorm bed, our friendship was drama free, purely cerebral. I figured that talking to him would help soften the drumbeat that kept me from thinking straight.

"Hey, Travis," I squeaked.

"Rachael, your voice sounds funny."

How could he tell? "Mom surprised Dad and me. She showed up at the house with her friend, Betts. Trudy and Sky were here. Everyone ate pot roast and broke bread. It was a big love fest."

"Was anyone poisoned or stabbed with a sharp utensil?"

I smiled. He thought I was a magnet for trouble. "Not yet. There was a fireball, but Dad extinguished it before the picnic table turned into embers."

"Sky? Does Trudy have a dog? And is your mom over this psychic thing?"

A growl vibrated my words. "No and no."

"Explain. And go slow."

"Sky is Trudy's younger sister. And Mom still claims to be receiving clairvoyance."

"Did she have any premonitions?"

"Nothing moving or life altering was uttered. No apologies or explanations. She and her mystic obsession are in town for a psychic expo. Apparently you can make a living telling people what they want to hear."

"She brought the psychic she ran away with to your house? Are you kidding?"

"I wish."

"Is there something you're not telling me?"

I picked at the cording on the pillowcase cover. Since I left home for college, a higher than normal amount of fakers had screwed around with my life, messing with my plans. In one breath, I blurted, "I'm pretty sure Mom's friend is her girlfriend. My gaydar is flashing. I think she switched camps."

The phone went quiet. I took a drag.

"Are you okay with that?" he asked.

Exhaling smoke out the window, I felt the night's bleakness wrap around my heart. "No, I'm not okay. She raised me traditionally, blissfully naive. Now she's gone alternative. I can't handle images of them spooning and kissing and—doing stuff. I thought I could be cool about her psychic pursuits, but she keeps dropping new bombs that I can't digest. And her girlfriend, she reads tarot cards, auras, and is a follower of Nostradamus. She's a freak, like someone you pay to view inside a carnival tent."

"Rach, relax. Your mom is discovering things about herself that she thinks are important. As much as you have trouble swallowing the new her, you need to, or you'll lose her. Besides, it couldn't get any worse. I mean she's dropped the biggest bomb there is. Right?"

"I could use some company. What are you doing for July Fourth weekend?"

"You want me to stay at the O'Briens' house of dysfunction?"

"You're a calming force. Can you drive up and visit for a few days?"

"I should be able to swing it."

NOTE TO SELF

I have a premonition this won't be an ordinary summer.

Flambé fiasco. Whoever thought it was a nifty idea to set food on fire?

I would've liked to be pleasantly surprised, and dead wrong, regarding my predetermined imagery of Betts. That didn't happen.

Asking Dad for permission to have Travis stay over Fourth of July. Must use cunning and choose the moment wisely. Yeah, right. How the hell am I going to convince Dad to let him stay with us?

4

Electrical Storm

A tin chandelier radiated light across the farm table, reflecting the dings and nicks under the varnish. Seating in our kitchen was an eclectic mix, and no two chairs matched. Dad's favorite was a high-back upholstered in velvet. After being on his feet and bending over a worktable during the day, he'd take two aspirin and rest his lower back against a heating pad. An auction guide and a pile of mail lay sprawled in front of him. I brought him cold can number two of Iron City Beer. As he popped the top, I leaned into the back frame of a Shaker chair and strategized my approach.

Being nineteen was dodgy. No longer a child, I still needed permission for Travis to visit. It's not like I could hide him for four days—not easily, anyway. I determined that a direct approach would be best, but waited until Dad swallowed enough gulps of beer. When he neared the bottom, I ambushed. "Could a friend of mine who's a boy visit for the Fourth of July weekend?"

Midswallow he unnaturally jerked. "This weekend? What boy?"

"One I met in North Carolina. His name is Travis, and he lives in Kentucky."

Dad pushed his auction guide aside. With his alert detection turned on high, he tightened his eyelids and contorted his mouth.

Initiating damage control, I clarified. "He's not a boyfriend. Just a friend."

"Rachael, any boy that drives from Kentucky to Canton will be looking for more than friendship."

My tongue brushed across my crooked eyetooth and I hiccupped. Placing a hand on Dad's, I patted down his concern. "Trust me. Travis is a friend."

He didn't look convinced, and I hesitated. I hadn't told anyone about Travis being gay. "His preference for romance falls in the same category as Mom's."

Dad grimaced. "He likes older women?"

Steadying eye contact, I said, "Dad, he's gay."

Polishing off the last few drips from the bottom of the can, he went silent for a beat. "We're tight on space with Trudy in the house."

I picked at furniture polish stains on my palm. "I noticed."

Our normally meticulous home had exploded with medicine balls, jump ropes, and a Suzanne Somers's Thigh Master. The butcher-block island was a clutter of herbal bottles with funky names like bilberry fruit, wormwood, and black walnut hull. They reminded me of ingredients for a witch's brew, and I had vowed not to consume anything Trudy offered.

Dad put the tab top inside his can and rattled it. "I agreed to let your mom and her friend stay in the studio above the shop."

"I'm surprised you're okay with that."

His eyes closed. "I don't know what I'm okay with anymore."

"No one's at Trudy's; maybe Travis could stay there. If she okays it."

Coming to terms with his estranged wife paying a surprise visit had sputtered and clunked the gears in Dad's head, sending the life he'd adjusted to without her amuck. Now Mom and her "girlfriend" were in Canton for a celestial summer of horoscope plotting, levitation, and channeling. Neither Dad nor I knew how to react. On the plus side, the complicated female dynamics in our lives weakened his normally regimented focus on rules and regulations.

I had an ulterior motive for having Travis stay at Trudy's that I didn't mention to Dad. In addition to providing me with cerebral solace, I thought he and I could kibosh the tidy thief folklore. If he stayed there without incident, we could convince Dad and Trudy that the apartment was safe for habitation, giving Dad and me some elbowroom to adjust to my gypsy mom.

"When's this boy coming?" Dad asked.

I bear-hugged his neck. "You're gonna love Travis."

EDMOND PUT THE SOLDERING gun down and took off his protective glasses. The garden design of the Tiffany chandelier hanging above our heads reflected the gleam of the overhead light, and blocks of color danced on the worktable. Green-saturated hues that mixed in darks and lights reminded me of the pond behind our house before dawn when sleepy daylight woke the grasses and reflected the algae that clung to its perimeter.

Midway through freshman year, my shoulder had dislocated when I fell out of a handcrafted milk crate dorm loft bunk onto linoleum. Besides a small lump on my collarbone that never went away, it had healed but left one odd quirk. The muscles near my shoulder sensed stormy weather. I didn't need the weatherman to tell me it was going to rain. My dodgy shoulder had become as precise a predictor as a barometer, and as the day progressed, the ache had strengthened.

By midafternoon, gusty breezes bounced the underside veins of the aged buckeye tree leaves in front of O'Brien's How's Your Art, and above, thick gray clouds collided as an approaching darkness engulfed the sky. A strike of lightning cracked. Like the rolling storm, my mind was turbulent, and I struggled with the knowledge that my mother had released her sexuality and that it favored her feminine side. If she was in love with Betts, causing a rift would be tricky.

Dad had left to give an estimate on a scratched dining table caused by the owner's daughter sliding a heavy twig basket across its surface. When distant thunder rumbled, Edmond and I moved to stand between the workshop's open barn doors.

I taxed a large quantity of brain cells in an attempt to spin the "new her" positively. Maybe Mom would encourage me to find my soul mate, and I began to formulate a side agenda—asking her to take me for my first gynie visit, but I hadn't come up with a smooth approach. When I returned to college, I was going to lose my virginity, and I figured I needed to be on birth control for when the moment struck.

Edmond and I enjoyed our break and continued to watch the horizon.

"The Tiffany is exquisite. Who brought it in?"

He drew a finger across his chin. "Geneva."

"Geneva McCarty?" I snorted. "Does Dad know?"

Rubbing at the calluses on the underside of his palm, he shrugged.

Nearby, the sky erupted with a rumble. I wrinkled my nose. "You and I both know they don't get along. If their shopping carts passed inside the Valu-King, they wouldn't speak. If he finds out we're restoring something for her, he'll go mental."

Like eagle feathers, the layered clouds moved swiftly, and my mind raced, dislodging my earliest memory of Geneva. Before the holidays—I must've been five or six—she had rung our doorbell. Mom and I were busy icing the wall of a gingerbread house. I devoured the purple gumdrop chimney while Mom answered the door. "Geneva?" her voice cracked.

Dressed in an icing-covered apron that matched Mom's, I peered around a corner at the open front door. With whirling snow behind her, she stepped past my mother and into our foyer. Geneva handed me a brown-paper-wrapped package. It was heavy and square, like a book. "I want your daddy to have this, and someday it will be yours."

Mom wiped her hands on her apron. "I'll see that John gets it."

Before Geneva left, she said, "It's something that should be kept in the family. Somewhere safe." Cupping my chin in her fur-gloved hand, she winked. Mom closed the door behind her and took the package from me, placing it on Dad's rolltop desk. While she poured herself some brandy from a bottle in the kitchen pantry, I snuck over and placed the package under the tree.

A boom thundered close by. "Work pays the bills. Besides," he said, patting my back, "we have extra help for the summer. Repairing that chandelier gives you experience with grinding glass and soldering."

"What happened between them, anyway? I mean Geneva is at least thirty years older than Dad. Did they have—relations?"

Edmond rattled his head. "Rachael."

"With the whole Trudy thing and all, I thought maybe Dad—you know."

"Phooey."

A fat raindrop fell on my cheek, then another on my shoulder. "Did a check bounce? Or did we screw up a painting for her, or what?"

The wind swayed branches, threatening to shake loose leaves into a shower of confetti. "It isn't my business, how it all started."

"Come on, Edmond, I'm nineteen. What's the big secret?"

Supersized raindrops splattered the pavers and in seconds turned into a downpour. We stepped back. He slid the barn doors closed, leaving them cracked open just a few inches. "It's not my place."

NOTE TO SELF
Travis's accommodations have been secured. YAY!

Geneva McCarty. Is she the client from hell, and Dad just doesn't want to deal, or is there something more?

I'm a big girl. If I'm going to do the deed, I need to take precautionary heed. Do medical tables really come equipped with stirrups?

5

Pesky Annoyances

Erratic weather with heavy rainfall was predicted to roll across the state for two more days. A cold spring had delayed the planting of the Ohio corn crop. The precipitation was received with delight by Edmond, an avid gardener, and the farmers who'd yet to harvest. Not only did the rain provide much-needed water, but would also drown the small larva of the European corn borer, a pesky moth that threatened to devastate the maturing crop from Massachusetts to Central Ohio. I had my own troubles and would've liked the storms to wash them away, but knew I had to rely on more than weather to get rid of Mom's and Dad's girlfriends.

After dinner, a quick burst of sun gleamed on the puddles that collected where the paths and driveways sagged. Peeling back my bedroom curtain, I watched for Sky. She and I had arranged to spend some time together to discuss the future demise of Trudy and Dad's relationship, or at the very least how to get them in separate living quarters. And she had volunteered to help me brainstorm ideas on how to persuade my mom that her Betts hobby was unhealthy.

Dad thought I'd be sleeping at Sky's, which was true-ish. Trudy lived in an apartment complex called Lakeside Shores, and Sky had a copy of her key. Sky's roommate had her boyfriend staying over, and they wanted alone-time, so tonight we'd stay at Trudy's and devise a plan to save the summer.

When I saw Sky drive up the street, I stuffed a twenty and a lip gloss into my pocket, grabbed my overnight bag, and shouted, "Bye, Dad."

He stood at the bottom of the stairs and ran a dishrag over an antique Satsuma vase.

I smiled and waited for the usual round of questions. *What were my plans? What time would I be home?*

"I think it's great that you and Sky are friends. Have a good time."

I waited.

He gave me a hug.

No inquisition. Weird. Did Dad want private time with Trudy? EUGH.

A SMALL BOATHOUSE RESTED on the edge of a man-made lake in the center of a cluster of apartment buildings. Cherry-red and ocean-blue paddleboats with white seats bobbed on ropes that were tethered to a dock. Eight of them were aligned like Bomb Pops in the lake that everyone at the complex called "the donut." Sky thought it looked more like a toilet seat with a patchy mound of grass full of goose crap in the middle. She called it "the commode."

Thunder rumbled above the parking lot, and in the twilight a gust of wind blew rain off wet leaves. I should've felt guilty about crashing at Trudy's without her permission, but rationalized that she'd committed a worse violation of space invasion to me at our house.

Before I scooted out of Sky's black 1975 Trans Am, she nudged me.

"What?" I asked.

Craning her neck heavenward, she cracked her shoulders. "Be on the lookout for some live space action tonight. I'm on call."

Indulging her, I glanced at the sunset. I didn't see anything that I'd classify as alien. Across a porcelain-blue backdrop, golden bursts intermingled with pink, reminding me of sand art. As a kid, I went through a phase of siphoning colored sand into decorative bottles. I'd concentrate on layering the silky-smooth colors so they didn't mix, but that never happened. My creations always became jumbled. I needed Sky to focus on earthlings. We had to come up with a solid roadblock that would press between Dad and Trudy's thing.

I hid an eye roll. She'd already given me an earful about her alien fascination. I'd made the mistake of asking if she honestly believed in extraterrestrials or if she was just enamored by the cute alien in the movie *ET*. She'd scoffed, shredding the movie improbabilities to pieces—the lack of extraterrestrial dialogue, planet origins, spaceship details, and a conversion of time travel. Then she spent twenty minutes trying to convince me to join MUFON, the Mutual UFO Network.

Had Sky and Trudy been abducted at some point? That would explain some of their oddities, clothing being at the top of the list. Sky religiously dressed in black or orange—one or the other, never mixing the two. Orange was her uniform color behind the juice bar counter at work, and black was for all other occasions. Tonight she wore monochromatic black jeans, a Flash Dance-esque off-the-shoulder t-shirt, and burnout boots. She and Trudy floated in antifashion bubbles.

I'm not a sci-fi fan, and my interest in the buffoonery of running around the state to log supposed UFO sightings, or manning phones for emergency calls, was zip. Unless there was the possibility of being abducted by a hot spaceman, she had no chance of recruiting me as a MUFON member. Using directional tactical questioning, I averted the alien topic. "Which building does Trudy live in?"

"Nineteen." She twittered her fingers. "Symbolizes the harmony and knowledge acquired by the sun and the moon."

The numerology mumbo crap that she shoveled caused my left eyebrow to arch. She was a bullshit artist, which on some level I admired.

Knowing Trudy, I had a predisposed idea of her apartment décor and was curious to see what "the clean thief" had done to make her bolt. When she'd called the police, they'd taken a look at her apartment, but since nothing had been stolen, they said there wasn't anything they could do. Clean and dusted, Trudy categorized the intrusion under vandalism. The officer told her that tidying didn't count as a prosecutable offense.

THE FINGER ROOTS OF a willow tree stretched beyond its draping canopy and had shifted the sidewalk in front of building nineteen. I tripped on uneven pavement. Sky steadied my arm. Tonight would help decompress my emotional upheaval and put a plan of action into place to bring some normalcy to my orbit.

A juniper bush holding a rifle jumped in front of us. My feet moved into auto-drive, and I bolted behind the nearest car. Sky jumped back and froze in front of the leaf-covered Sasquatch. He'd been hiding in the shrubs that choked a lamppost. At last count, I'd had three restraining orders issued, and it wasn't improbable that Billy Ray, his cousin Jack, or Bridget Bodsworth had come to pop my clock.

Sky kicked Sasquatch in the shin.

"Jesus," he said, rubbing his ankle, "you don't need to be so violent."

I peeked above the hood. Markus Doneski was no Sasquatch. He was a fuckup whose gene pool included the gift of annoyance. I'd spent an entire semester of trigonometry with his fingers flicking my back while he spewed a litany of vulgar commentary under his breath.

As I stepped out from behind the car, he pointed at me and laughed.

I didn't know if he lived in this apartment complex and didn't care. Assholes, I realized, are a lot like freckles. They stick with you, and some even grow bigger over time. Drawing a fast bird, I told him, "Eat shit and die."

His fake pout flexed the blond peach fuzz above his lip. He tipped the lid of his twig-covered baseball hat. "O'Brien, aren't you going to introduce me?"

My eyes lasered Doneski in an attempt to incinerate the annoying essence of his presence.

Sky stepped forward and reached out a hand, "Sorry about nailing your shin. My self-defense kicked into auto." She introduced herself. "Sky Bleaux."

The corners of his mouth twitched, and he attempted a macho head nod. Retrieving a partially used cigarette from behind his ear, he put it in his mouth. "Markus."

Doneski was lanky with feathered blond hair. I didn't categorize him as fit or unfit. His physique was the only thing normal about him. He eyed our duffel bags. "Planning a slumber party?"

My shoulder bag dropped to the ground. "Don't you have anything better to do than hide in the bushes?"

"Light?" he asked.

Sky reached in her pocket and tossed him a disposable Bic. After flicking it, he handed the lighter back and raised his gun, which alarmed me. Doneski was like a jumping jack firecracker. He had a short fuse and was unpredictable. It was only a matter of time before he was arrested; I just hadn't settled on the exact illegal endeavor he'd choose.

"Night like this, you never know what's lurking. I can give you a discount rate for my protection."

"Give me that," I said and snatched the firearm loose from his arm. After emptying the BB ammo into the grass, I shoved it into his chest. "Grow up, Doneski. We're not interested in playing cops and robbers with you."

"For your information, I don't just shoot BBs." He rocked forward onto his toes. "I'm a member of BBFA."

"What's that?" Sky asked.

"Big Bangers' Firearm Association."

Sky let out a snort, and I laughed in my throat.

Linking my arm into Sky's, I pulled her toward building nineteen. Over my shoulder I shouted, "Try not to shoot your big banger on your way home."

Doneski clicked a fresh cartridge of BBs into his gun. "Call me if you get scared."

Sky opened the lobby door.

"Markus is a perv," I said.

We peered out of the building's glass doors as the sunset vanished on the horizon. "He's gone, but we could have another encounter." She dug into her pocket for Trudy's key chain. "Full moon. That's lunar cuisine for extraterrestrials. Activity will significantly spike over the next four days."

The light that reflected off the floor-to-ceiling metallic-silver seventies wallpaper created a yellow and orange optical illusion of movement. If you stared at it too long, your eyes would cross and a cluster headache could ignite. Rubbing my temples, I closed my eyes. "Sky, I don't believe in spaceships and little green men."

Thinking of Doneski and his BB gun, I didn't feel threatened. He'd do anything for attention, and this was one of his antics. Just like in high school, I incinerated the encounter from my head.

I followed Sky up a set of open-back stairs. "Which apartment?"

"Top floor. Three C, at the back."

The hallway we walked along had been fumigated with lily-of-the-valley carpet freshener. A lock clicked. It sounded like Doneski's BB gun, and we spun around. Three doors behind us, a woman carried a trash bag toward the staircase. Her braided hair wound on top of her head like a pillbox hat. She hummed nonsense words. "Ocha kiniba, cheke."

"Hi, Mrs. Curtis," Sky said before slipping the key into Trudy's door lock.

Squinting at the two of us, Mrs. Curtis pulled the garbage bag backward. She tightened her lip above her teeth and froze like a bowler preparing for a strike.

Waving her hands in a windshield wiper blade motion, Sky said, "Remember me? Trudy's sister, Sky Bleaux."

Mrs. Curtis adjusted her frameless granny glasses. Her face relaxed, and she moved toward us. "You startled me. I mean, with all the robberies in town, you just can't be too careful. Two apartments in building seven, cleaned out. Where is Trudy? I haven't seen her in weeks. Teaching all those aerobic classes, I hope she hasn't strained any of her woman parts."

"All her parts are fine," Sky said.

Last time I spoke to Trudy, her brain parts were definitely strained.

"She's been staying with—er—a friend," Sky explained. "This is Rachael."

Mrs. Curtis's hand quivered. Reaching out, she clasped the eye of Horus that hung on a chain around my neck. Closing her eyes she chanted baby babble. "Ooch, eech—ah—ah—ah—eke, eke."

Sky grinned.

I held back a giggle.

"It must be the moon," Sky said, sending me into a knee bender spasm of laughter.

My parents taught me to be respectful toward teachers, neighbors, and clients. Basically, anyone ten years older than me, and I've only broken that rule of etiquette twice: when I met Trudy and now giggling in front of Mrs. Curtis.

The chanting slowed. She released my trinket, and her eyes popped open. "Well, do tell Trudy I miss her company." From down the hall, she said, "Be safe. Ophiuchus is in its rising phase." She carried the garbage bag back into her apartment, and we heard her lock click.

"Ophiuchus?" I asked.

Sky pushed Trudy's door open. "The thirteenth zodiac sign."

"Have you been hanging out with my mom and Betts or something?"

She stiffened. "My hobby is planetary movement, constellations, and black holes. I don't see colors around people, and I've never felt that I could prophesize. But I keep an open mind."

"Don't keep your mind too open, or you may end up like Mrs. Curtis. Did you see her eyelids flap open?"

"Hair wrapped like that is bound to turn off some circuitry. She needs to loosen her braids."

Inside Trudy's, I walked across a gym mat, careful not to stub a toe on a set of barbells. Over the past weeks, our house had acquired features similar to Trudy's apartment. "You have to help me get your sister to move out," I told Sky. "She pesters me to exercise and keeps asking if I'm coming to her ten o'clock."

Biting her lip, Sky made a sympathetic grimace.

Plastic storage boxes were stacked into a pyramid on a dining room table, and a sofa and chairs rested somewhere below jars of glitter, boxes of mismatched silverware, chipped plates, buttons, and doorknobs. It shouldn't have surprised me. Trudy was a junker.

Sky went into Trudy's bedroom and came back with two bottles of Lambrusco.

I raised a questioning eyebrow.

"Trudy doesn't drink. These were left over from a New Year's party. She'll never notice."

She found drinking glasses in the hall closet and handed one to me.

"I thought the tidying thief had been here. Why does Trudy have all this stuff?"

Settling into a corner chair, Sky said, "I have a theory. The tidying thief wasn't from planet earth."

The Lambrusco was sweet like fizzy grape juice, and I felt my muscles relax. "It's obvious. Trudy concocted that story so she could move in with my dad."

Sky finished her glass and poured another. "No offense, but your dad and Trudy. That's just—not right."

Glancing out the balcony slider door, I checked to see if Doneski was still under the shrubbery.

Sky removed her boots. "There's one question we need to answer."

"This better not involve intergalactic travel," I warned.

Widening her eyes, she twirled a strip of orange hair around a finger. "We need to figure out if it's the sex or emotional fulfillment? Once we know the big picture, we can concentrate on chipping away at it."

I filled my cup to the brim. "We don't need to analyze the details. We just need a plan to separate them."

From inside a pant pocket, she pulled out a joint and wiped lint off it. Flicking her Bic, she waved me toward her. Smoking happy grass was the best problem-solving suggestion she'd come up with. Inhaling was bound to trigger ideas.

"We could pay someone to hit on Trudy," I squeaked. "Like a body builder from the gym."

Mulling that over, Sky shrugged without enthusiasm.

"I know," Sky said. "Why don't we plant a bottle of Lindane shampoo in your dad's shower?"

"What's that?" I asked.

She giggled. "Prescription shampoo for crabs."

I wasn't buzzed enough to think that was a smart idea. "They'd think it was mine." I took the last hit before the paper disintegrated. "The perfect solution would be one that happened naturally."

The pot smoke diffused Sky's self-censoring, and the words she spoke had sharp edges. "Like your mom and dad getting back together?"

I rubbed the eye of Horus that rested on my neck.

"Have your parents been seeing one another?"

"Not really," I confessed. "Mom's been busy hanging out with Betts, getting ready for the psychic expo. I've only seen the PUs—parental units—together once."

"Maybe they're working things out," Sky said.

I slumped on top of a rumpled quilt that covered the sofa. "I don't think so. Yesterday in the shop, we heard furniture moving in the studio loft. Dad went upstairs to see what was going on. When he came back down his face was red. He said something about Mom and Betts improving the energy flow. As far as I can tell my parents are barely speaking."

Sky licked her pointer finger and held it up. "Maybe we're looking at this all wrong. We need to get rid of the interference."

"Interference?" Unsure if Sky had digressed into the MUFON lingo, I slid open the balcony door and let fresh after-rain air into the apartment.

"If Betts believed your mom threatened to reveal insider information on the psychic thing—and if your mom became mad at Betts for questioning her loyalty—their alliance could be shaken. And with your mom back in town without psychic ties..." Sky shrugged. "You know."

"Know what?"

"Your dad's romance with my sister would become difficult."

The sliding door curtains billowed around me, making me appear ghostly. "You may have something. But can we pull it off?"

"As long as Betts isn't psychic we can."

"She's not psychic," I said with sudden insight, "unless you consider psychics masters at exposing vulnerability."

"Maybe it's time someone played on hers," Sky said.

The night was quiet until the noisy raindrops began to spat when they hit the deck. The damp air drew goose bumps on my skin. I felt naughty, but what choice did I have? It was time for some reverse karma. I'd have to do some snooping and carefully choose the words I spoke to Mom and Betts. *It could work.*

Lighting a cigarette, I watched a white van with a dented bumper stop at a building diagonally across the street. A figure with a twig hat jogged in front of the headlights and got into the passenger side. We didn't need to worry about Markus Doneski. He had other plans, and so did I. I rubbed my tongue over my crooked eyetooth. The Psychic and Paranormal Expo should be enlightening.

NOTE TO SELF

Don't open kelp powder. Smells like cat piss and may contain microbes that encourage you to wear excessive amounts of neon spandex.

Betts's removal—wish I could just call an exterminator.

6

Enlightenment

My shoulder stopped aching, but my head was pounding. I didn't feel motivated to upholster the seats of the chairs I'd been restoring. Besides the Lambrusco and the residual pot that punished my brain, the client's fabric selection—muddied orange velvet—launched waves of nausea up my throat. *Thank God Dad wasn't in this morning.* There was a high probability that I'd lose my breakfast.

Since it was the Saturday before the Fourth of July, Edmond and I were only working until two. Travis was on the road, and he planned to be at my house by three.

Although Travis and I talked on the phone all the time, I hadn't seen him since we'd slept together, in the literal, nonromantic sense. I thought he'd be "the one," but turns out I'm attracted to gay men. With no chance of getting naked with him, I'd settled for his friendship. Because of a few minor incidents freshman year—falling out of a loft while intoxicated, being run over by a frenemy, shagging a three-step with a demented art forger, and being held at gunpoint by a wackadoo—he thinks my life is an action-packed riot. *A complete overassumption.* Regardless, I tolerate his self-perceived normalcy in exchange for his cut-through-the-crap insight.

I hadn't told him all my plans for this weekend. An uneventful night at the psychic expo would prove that my life is truly dull, but with his company I hoped we'd manage a few giggles.

Laying the crushed orange velvet on the cutting table, I winced.

"What are you doing this weekend?" I asked Edmond.

"Lake O' Pines."

"In the bullet on wheels?"

He smiled and nodded. I wished I were the one road-tripping in a knock-it-until-you-rock-it refurbished 1965 Airstream Safari romance-mobile. This summer had no promise of a hookup for me, but I hoped it would unearth something I could use to eradicate Betts.

Edmond answered the phone while I fiddled with pinning a paper pattern on the fabric.

He hung up. "I'm going to Geneva McCarty's. She wants me to look at a painting. Wanna come?"

"Should we tell Dad?"

"Naw. He's at Gert's. Her air-conditioner is on the fritz."

My mind was not in upholstery mode. A sales call would be a welcome distraction. The visit to Geneva's would be a quick in and out. Afterward, I needed to get back to the shop and make nice with Mom. I hadn't patched things up since the flambé-lesbian fiasco at our house. If I wanted her back in my life, I'd have to smooth out the prickly edges that made our recent conversations difficult.

Edmond dangled the van keys. "You can drive."

GENEVA MCCARTY LIVED IN a fairy tale Hansel and Gretel Tudor with neatly aligned slate roof tiles and drooping gables. The exterior was sandstone cut from a local quarry. An art studio, greenhouse, and storage shed nestled within the forest that surrounded her estate. With my foot off the gas, I glided down her driveway, passing half a dozen black iron lampposts. I'd been to her home a few times, but never with Dad.

The last time I was here, a year ago, Edmond and I picked up a Japanese silk shoji screen that had torn. A twang of guilt strummed along my veins. At some point, something had gone wrong between Dad and Geneva. She didn't seem overly difficult to me, but what did I know? When I read her customer file on Dad's desk, I realized she'd been a client since before I was born. If she was a royal pain in the dunkus, I wondered why we continued to conduct business with her.

Edmond pushed the black button that rested inside an ornate scroll design on the front door, and we waited.

"Are you sure she's expecting us today?" I asked.

Knocking loudly, he shouted, "Hello, Geneva."

I stood with my back to the door and looked at the rolling mounds of buffalo grass that carpeted the ground between aged maple trees. This storybook lawn was lush, devoid of dandelions, thistle weeds, or patches of clover. Everything about Geneva McCarty seemed well kept.

"Hello, Edmond," Geneva shouted from twenty feet away. Wearing brightly colored pedal pushers and a halter top, she waved from the doorway of her tempered glass orchid house. Her garden-gloved hand set a pair of pruners inside a bucket she carried. "So sorry, I was repotting some Phalaenopsis and lost track of time."

"Not to worry," Edmond said, waiting for her to meet us before kissing her on both her cheeks.

"Rachael, dear," she said. "It's lovely to see you. Your hair looks lighter. Have you been in the sun?"

She was always so perceptive about me. I guessed I reminded her of her youth. "A little."

"The coloring suits you. Come in and have a cup of tea."

Geneva was born in the UK, and although her accent had softened from years spent in Ohio, she still considered herself a Geordie. Edmond turned the stove top on and pulled out the cups and saucers while she led me to the summer porch.

"So how was your first year at college? Did you learn anything?"

"A few things," I said.

"Did you meet anyone interesting?"

That was an understatement.

"What's his name, or is there more than one?"

I felt my face flush. *Actually three, if I were honest.*

"Oh go on and tell me. Give me something other than orchids and creaky joints to talk about."

Relenting information, I said, "There's a guy." I checked the doorway, not wanting Edmond to overhear. "Clay Sorenson."

She sat in a corner wicker chair and opened her cigarette box.

"He's southern. Studying physical therapy."

"Are you in love?"

Jeez, Geneva.

"Ladies," Edmond mused as he set down a tray and poured tea from an oriental blue teapot. "Now, what needs to be repaired?"

She squeezed a lemon slice. "*Cassandra.*"

"Of Troy?" I asked.

"I had a fresh coat of paint applied in the study," she said before drawing a sip, "and when the painting was removed from the wall, I noticed a residue buildup on the rocks below her feet. She looks dull."

Edmond crossed his legs at the ankle and blew on the steam that rose from his cup. "We'll take her back to the shop—brighten her up."

A wooden cigarette box with a worn indentation near the lid rested on her lap. Sliding her fingers inside, she pinched a dark brown Indonesian Kretek cigarette and rolled it between her fingers. "How's the Tiffany?"

"You won't recognize it. The leaded glass arrived. Rachael has been helping me cut and grind the pieces and solder them into place."

"Have you, love?"

I set my cup down. "The chandelier is killer."

She fitted the unlit cigarette into a jewel-encrusted holder. "I fought for that lamp."

"In a bar brawl?" I asked, recalling a freshman encounter.

Geneva and Edmond laughed.

"Practically. I won it at the Carnegies'."

"Poker?" I asked.

Edmond moved to flick a lighter for her. As she inhaled through the lipstick-stained holder, the cloves inside the ragged paper cracked. *I so craved a drag.*

"I used dexterity and cunning in a strategy." With a cluck of her tongue, she winked. "Mixed the whisky sours myself before a friendly lawn bowling tournament."

Edmond and I howled. Geneva McCarty was an eccentric hoot, and I enjoyed hearing about her shenanigans, but this was taking a while. I looked at my Swatch. We'd been away from the shop longer than I'd expected. Moving things along, I asked, "Where's the painting?"

With a firm, practiced hand, she stubbed out her cigarette butt and stood. "Come on, I'll show you."

The walls in the study emitted a newly painted fumy scent. Plate-size leaves of a grand oak tree swept against floor-to-ceiling paned window glass. Under a billow of wind, they lazily flapped like an awning. Even in the room's disarray, I imagined I could dally endless hours staring out of the window. But not today.

My eyes veered into a box of books at my feet, and I browsed titles. Some were in Latin, others French and Chinese. I read the spines: an Edgar Allan Poe intimately caressed the Grand Dame of Mystery, Agatha Christie. In between them, I ran my finger against a purple velvet case that covered a leather book jacket. "May I?" I asked.

"Of course." Her eyes sparked magic. "Are you a believer in prophecies?"

I wondered if she knew Betts. "I'm a believer in making my own prophecies."

Geneva and Edmond chortled. She turned her attention to him and watched as he snaked around boxes and folded tarps. The *Cassandra* painting leaned against the wall behind a French provincial desk, and I caught sight of the corner of an ornate gold-leafed frame. "Edmond, do be careful."

The book inside the velvet case had cracks in the grain and peeling leather. A string entwined a figure eight around two circular cutouts the size of shirt buttons, holding the jacket secure. The title read *d'Orus Apollo Des notes hieroglyphiques*, by Nostradamus. The loops in the gold-leaf lettering were familiar. I rewound my memory. Geneva had dropped it off at our house years ago for my father, and I'd hidden the wrapped gift under the Christmas tree. *What was it doing here? Holy shit, this is a freakin' relic. A first edition, and I'm not wearing gloves. Crap, the oils on my hands. I could be arrested by the museum police.*

I used the soft velvet case as a potholder and gripped the book by the spine. I didn't dare open it. "You know this looks like a rare edition of Nostradamus."

Geneva waved her hand around the room. "It's a book of epigrams. Nostradamus's translation of Horapollon of Manouthis. Are you familiar with the work?"

"Wasn't Horapollo one of the last leaders of ancient Egyptian priesthood at a school in Menouthis, near Alexandria, during the reign of Zeno? Like in 474–491 AD?"

Edmond crossed his arms and made a lousy attempt of holding in a smirk, while Geneva skirted her tongue across her upper teeth.

Edmond knew I had a photographic memory. Had he told Geneva? Both were versed in history, but I hadn't yet given them my head dump.

"He had to flee because he was accused of plotting a revolt against the Christians, and his temple to Isis and Osiris was destroyed," Edmond said.

"History books say that he was eventually captured and, after torture, converted to Christianity. Some believe him to be the author of hieroglyphics. This belongs under glass," I said.

Fluttering an arm over her head, Geneva said, "Books should be enjoyed." She surveyed the boxes. "I've been meaning to catalogue these before they go back on the shelf."

From across the room, Edmond lifted the gilded frame of the *Cassandra* for Geneva and me to see. Red locks of hair cascaded around a fair-skinned beauty in a blue sheath. "She who entangles men," he said.

"The very one," Geneva purred.

I wasn't a man, but her beauty snared me. Sliding the book I held back into its case, I made a mental note to ask Dad about it.

"Who's the artist?" I asked.

"Evelyn Pickering De Morgan," Edmond said.

Resting against a wall, Geneva lit up another cigarette she had tucked in a side table drawer. As she blew a plume into the air, I cringed, but didn't lecture her on the vices of smoking around six-figure artwork. "Painted before you were born," she mused.

"Eighteen ninety-eight," Edmond said.

Treading over boxes of books, I moved closer to Edmond. "The end of the Victorian era."

Geneva seemed lost in memories. "De Morgan was a forward thinker, woman's libber. She lived in the height of social and spiritual reform. Painted strong-minded females. Ones that personified spiritual empowerment."

"The yellow swags in her cloak depict sympathy," Edmond said.

I shifted my stance. "And the red roses at her feet, martyrdom."

Resting her elbows on a high-back chair, Geneva told us, "It was a time of renewed hope for women. De Morgan was an optimist, and her paintings reflected her pursuit of spiritualism."

"Some linseed oil and turpentine will remove the residue buildup," Edmond said.

"Do be careful. She's one of my favorites."

Edmond carried the *Cassandra* into the hallway. "We'll return her safe and sound."

"Rachael," Geneva said. "I wanted to discuss a matter with you. Actually, it's more of a project I have in mind."

AS I TURNED THE VAN down the private drive toward Dad's shop, I checked my watch. I had a half hour until Travis was due in town, barely enough time to get back to the house and change clothes.

My mind flitted. It was already July. Before I tapped the first domino in my plan to eliminate Betts and move Trudy out, I needed to broach a personal topic with my mother. Although my love interest from freshman year and I weren't conversing, I was an optimist, and I needed to secure birth control before I returned to campus in the fall. I clung to the fantasy that her new openmindedness would inspire her to aid me in the discovery of my sexual prowess. I didn't want Mom to be my girlfriend, and I wasn't up for sharing details. I just wanted her to help me protect myself from unwanted pregnancy.

"Expecting company?" Edmond asked.

I looked at the carport. "Travis!"

He stood next to his Volvo station wagon and chewed on an apple that he'd bitten down to the core. Leaping out, I wrapped myself around his neck, and he spun me with one arm. In a t-shirt and jeans, with a shaved face and a tan, he looked even better than I'd remembered.

A noisy June bug dive-bombed my ear and I ducked. "Have you been waiting long?"

"Twenty minutes."

"Sorry, I got hung up at—"

Edmond carried the *Cassandra* painting and held his free hand out.

"Travis Howard, this is Edmond."

"Pleasure," Travis said.

Edmond nodded.

"How did you know to find me here?"

"I met your dad at your house. He gave me directions."

Hoping Dad didn't say anything overly annoying, I flicked through the horseshoe key chain, and unlocked the barn door. Sliding it open, I stiffened.

"Mom?" She was with Betts. They hovered over a worktable in front of the Tiffany.

"How did you two get in?" Edmond asked sharply as he set *the Cassandra* on an easel.

I wondered the same thing. Last Christmas when it became clear that Mom wasn't coming back, Dad had rekeyed the locks at the house and the shop. If he were here, he'd be miffed.

Mom splayed her hand on the chest of a billowy three-quarter-sleeve sundress that swallowed her under pleats of fabric. "Oh, Edmond. You startled me. Betts wanted some advice on staining an old dresser." Mom pointed at the open door above the shop. "We came down the apartment stairs for a peek at the work floor."

Did Dad forget to rekey that door?

"Hello," Mom said to Travis.

"Travis, this is my mom and her—er—friend, Betts."

Mom became distracted. Not by Travis, but by the painting. "Oh, that's lovely. Who commissioned us?"

Us?

Edmond retrieved a folded cotton sheet and moved toward the painting. "Rachael and I just picked the piece up from Geneva's."

Mom furled her eyebrows, making a crease between them. "McCarty?" she whispered and stared at me.

Did she know something I didn't?

Moving in closer, Betts stroked the edges of the frame. "Cassandra of Troy?"

Having taken a Hellenistic Age elective that mostly focused on epic poems from Homer, the painting piqued Travis's interest and he walked toward it. "The daughter of King Priam and Queen Hecuba of Troy."

"Seems like everyone's familiar with Greek mythology," Edmond said.

Travis opened his mouth, but before he articulated words, Betts interrupted. "Passionately."

With Mom alone at the far end of the studio, I summoned my nerve and scurried toward her for an ambush while Betts, Edmond, and Travis became engrossed in analyzing the details of *Cassandra*. I cleared my throat. "Mom?" I whispered.

Cupping my chin, she smiled. "Yes, dear."

"I think I need a doctor's appointment."

She placed her palm on my forehead. "You're not running a fever. Is it your throat?"

"No, it's not my throat."

"Well then, what is it?"

"It's womanly," I said, louder than I meant to.

Mom's left eye twitched, and she blinked like she was sending Morse code with her eyelids. She shouted over to Edmond, "Betts is a historical connoisseur. She lived in Lyon while she studied arts and social sciences at the local university. Tell them, Betts. How you've traveled Europe, India, and Asia."

Using the old *pretend-I-didn't-hear-what-I-think-I-heard,* Mom sank my gynie appointment request to the ocean floor, and I didn't know if I had the resolve to revive my request. She'd never had the bird and bee talk with me. Maybe because she preferred girl birds nesting with girl birds, and the whole boy-meets-girl-happily-ever-after spiel never made sense to her. Making matters worse, it seemed she'd dropped a quarter into her animated friend's box of blabber.

Betts flicked her hands at an imaginary cloud that encircled the painting. "Cassandra inspired Apollo to grant her the gift of prophecy."

"Buckle up," I whispered to no one in particular.

Travis leaned back against a stool. "Some gift. No one believed her predictions. Her visions became a source of pain and frustration."

I met Edmond's twinkling eyes. My heart swelled. One point for Travis. *God, I wish he were straight.*

Betts twisted a red-marbled stone ring around her index finger. "Some of the most insightful people are misunderstood, ignored, or thought insane." Her eyes were fixed on the portrait. "Cassandra foresaw the Trojan horse, the death of Agamemnon, and her own murder at the hands of Clytemnestra and Aegisthus."

I picked up a paintbrush and swept splintered glass remnants that had scattered under the suspended Tiffany. "Her prophetic insight caused her to go insane. The translations of her visions have undoubtedly been altered after the fact." *Just like yours.*

"What are you saying?" my mom asked.

That your girlfriend likes the sound of her own words, I wanted to say, but I had a plan to stick to, so I softened my response. "Folklore has a way of making figures more insightful than they actually were."

Betts's enlarged eyes pierced into mine as if she could intimidate my mind.

"Are your eyes dry? Do you need some drops?" I asked, not wanting any more of her loose interpretations of mythology, especially with Travis visiting. He already thought I lured trouble. Seeing Betts morph into her mother-medium-ship-O-woohoo would only add fuel to his crazies-are-attracted-to-Rachael theory.

Betts pinched her thumbs and index fingers, and rolling her head back in a phony sorcerer warm up, she began slurring, "I'm feeling a presence—a change is inevitable."

Anger scorched my insides and left a charred taste in my mouth, like burnt oil. *No shit. It's called time, and it's irreversible.* I wanted Betts to take her con artist ass out of my realm, and go flap her marshmallow fluff at some other schmuck's family. How could Mom think this bullshit was real? And why was she subjecting Dad and me to this crap?

NOTE TO SELF
Geneva McCarty has a house full of treasure. In the short time I was there, my hands must have touched seven figures worth of furniture and rare edition books.

Travis witnessed the psychic show. Sorry he had to see the circus, but now he knows I'm not exaggerating about my mother and "her friend's" realm of reality.

7

Clairvoyance

My aunt Gert was a creature of habit. Her attire varied in color, but never in style. Even in the July heat, she wore matching sweat suit separates. Today she wore royal blue. The shade drew out her eyes and gave her an air of sovereignty.

Dad organized his toolbox while Travis chalked a cue stick and broke the rack.

Aunt Gert bent below the opening of her kitchen pass-through and rotated the antenna on her old-fashioned stand-up radio. It looked more like a wood trunk with dials than something meant to produce sound. She struggled to find a nonstatic station.

Gert wasn't my biological aunt, but I considered her family. She was my deceased maternal grandmother's lifelong friend and roommate of twenty years. Mom, Dad, and I had spent every holiday with her, except one. Last November, she won the raffle at the Bingo Bucket and chose a free weekend in Vegas over turkey with Dad and me.

Her new window air-conditioner motor churned in a battle against the late-afternoon heat. Chin up, arms out, Dad stood frozen in front of the unit like the letter *T* while Icelandic air shed relief on his sweat-stained armpits.

I wanted to have a conversation with Dad about Betts. After two wacko encounters, I was convinced she was a con artist. I just didn't know her playing field. I didn't think Mom had given her money, but I wasn't sure. What did my mother possess that would be of interest to Betts? I hoped it wasn't a kinky sex thing. I wasn't brave enough to delve there and had erected barricades in those dim mind avenues. My mom had become a dodgy topic that Dad avoided, too. Navigating a conversation about her would have to be approached with care.

Pleased with the spread of balls across the jeweled-purple felt pool table, Travis stepped aside and leaned against a wood-paneled wall. Aunt G fiddled with the radio until Rod Stewart asked if we thought he was sexy. Aunt G did and sang along. Moving toward us, she grazed the edges of the varnished oak pool table with her fingertips and winked at Travis. As for Travis, he was about to become a believer.

While smoking tobacco through a pipe, Aunt G made friendly hip contact with Travis's. Fidgeting with his hands, he kept his eyes on his shoelaces as he politely grappled with the bountiful basket of mojo that she launched at him. I had to smirk. He'd accused me of magnifying the finer personality quirks of my family, but now he was moments away from witnessing the Annie Oakley of pool. She was going to wallop his backside and, for an encore, spit shine the floor with it. It wouldn't be pretty.

With bent knees, Aunt G perched her apple ass out and rested her bountiful chest at the rail. She squinted her left eye as she pulsed a Panama cocobolo stick between her knuckles. Angling downward, she skipped the cue ball over a ten stripe and knocked a three solid into the corner pocket.

Travis's mouth gaped. "You've got to be kidding."

Gert patted him on the shoulder and moved to the side rail. She placed her back to the table and maneuvered her stick under her left arm to take out the orange five with one hand.

Travis rolled his eyes.

The solid two and six were aligned near the foot rail, and she made a show of sinking them both. Nudging Travis's shoulder with her stick, she asked, "Are you just takin' it easy on an old girl?"

Travis bent down and rubbed his hand beneath the table. "It has to be magnetized. Rachael probably has a remote in her pocket."

I patted my front and rear short pockets. "Sorry, nothing but denim."

Dad shook his head and told Travis, "Don't feel bad. I've never won a game. Go easy on the boy. I'm going home to get a clean shirt. Trudy and I will be back with dinner."

As soon as Dad's truck door slammed, Gert tapped my knee with her stick. "Cold suds are in the garage fridge. Why don't you get us all one? Help relax Travis's pool arm."

When I returned, she'd cleared the table. Travis collected the balls and asked her, "Will you show me how to shoot with my back to the table?"

Gert popped the cap off a green glass bottle and poured the Rolling Rock into a beer stein with a lid. She took a long swallow and told us, "It's simple geometry and positioning."

I held my ponytail up, letting chilled air dust the back of my neck. From a corner stool, I asked, "Have you seen Mom since she's been back?"

Hand rolling a ball across the table, she confessed, "I have."

Travis took a shot and scratched.

She lined up another and repositioned his grip.

"And?"

Aunt G took another swallow. "I love Maeve, but her fuse has shorted. And that Betts? She's a stinkbug. Doesn't miss a beat, asked me all about my pool table and cues, trying to butter me up."

"What's the attraction?" I asked.

Gert shook her head with enough vigor to rattle the knotted white bun that rested on the top of her head. "The Maeve I knew had a mind of her own, and I wonder where it's gone. I don't know what she's thinking, hovering in that woman's shadow."

Aunt G adjusted Travis's shoulders and stepped aside. He made contact with the cue ball but missed the pocket.

With my finger, I traced the white 33 on the Rolling Rock bottle. The printed number was a mistake on the initial run. Supposedly it represented the label's word count and wasn't meant to be printed. But someone made a mistake, and with the Depression, it would've been too costly to correct. The misprint ended up becoming a trademark whose origin had sparked outlandish intoxicated theories. I hoped Betts wouldn't become the 33 in our family. I already wanted to forget her. "Betts makes a living trancing out and telling people about themselves."

Gert scoffed. "People paying hard-earned money for someone to tell them a fortune. I could save them their shekels and dole out free wisdom. Get off your keister and make life happen."

Travis choked his stick and released. He ricocheted the ball across the table and into a bumper. It rolled back and tapped a solid into a side pocket. Gert and I cheered.

The temperature inside the bungalow began to drop. Sliding my flip-flops off, I hugged my knees. "I'm going to get Mom away from Betts. But I'm not sure how to lift the fog out of her head."

"Things would have to be posed to her in a nonconfrontational manner. On her turf," Gert said.

Tapping her fingers under her chin, she smiled at Travis.

I liked her subtle suggestion and stared as well.

He stepped back. "Me? I just met your mom."

I sipped my beer. "You have a gift of subtlety."

Aunt G told Travis, "Maeve would never suspect an outsider."

"Oh no. Forget it. I don't do confrontation. This is a bad idea."

Dad walked in through the front door holding a bucket of fried chicken, and Trudy trailed him carrying the sides. "What's a bad idea?"

IT WAS THE MAGICAL time of the evening when the sun swept low. The sky relinquished a darkening drop cloth that closed in on a final burst of showy brights. I expected psychic expo attendees to drive rusters, hippie vans, and campers. Travis parked his Volvo station wagon between a Mercedes Benz 560 and a Chevy Camaro. This wasn't as hillbilly a scene as I'd thought it would be.

My game needed to be on. I was over Betts's intrusion into my family. She was slippery, and being in the same room with her sent my alarm bells and whistles off. I wanted to know how she really made a living. I doubted it was on the up and up. Once I had a handle on what I was dealing with, I hoped I could talk some sense into Mom.

Travis wore Adidas sweats and a t-shirt. Wanting to blend with the crowd in case undercover work transpired, I'd tied a mademoiselle scarf around my head, and although I normally didn't bother with much more than mascara and lip gloss, I'd spent considerable time applying makeup. I batted my Cleopatra eyes at Travis. "Too much?"

"Where's your crystal ball?"

"I knew I forgot something."

He leaned against his car while I fumbled in my jacket pocket for a cigarette. Dad's vices consisted of Iron City Beer and his Trudy habit. Other than those, he was squeaky clean. My moments away from him were few, and when the opportunity presented itself, I indulged in a slim Benson & Hedges.

"We were lucky to find a parking space. I thought this would be some rinky-dink, small-time carnival," Travis said.

I exhaled downwind. "They've advertised it in the local papers and on billboards all over town."

Travis started to walk. "Trudy seemed interested in all the natural healing stuff. Do you think she'll show up tonight?"

"And potentially bump into my mom? Compare notes about Dad? Not a chance."

"Did you tell your mom we were coming?"

"No. I've barely had two minutes alone with her since she's been back."

"Your dad was cool about us coming."

"Only because I guilted him."

"Trudy helped. Saying she thought it would be harmless to take a look around. Her approval convinced him."

"She only said that to suck up to me."

"Why?"

I made a show of an eye roll. "She's wants to be my 'friend.'"

Sparse islands of trees and shrubbery dotted the parking lot. Travis and I dallied in one of the asphalt oases while I finished my ciggie. "Are you ready for this?" he asked.

Stubbing out my butt, I motioned forward. "As ready as I'll ever be."

The entrance fee for two was twelve dollars. I handed a guy inside a glass booth a twenty, gratis of Dad. At a second set of doors, a ticket collector with hawk feathers embellished on top of her head rested a hand against a carved cane. Travis held out our tickets. The towering headpiece distracted me, and I didn't immediately recognize the beehive of twisted braids under the feathery cap.

"Mrs. Curtis?"

"I knew our paths would cross. Ophiuchus is still rising. I hope you haven't run into any trouble?"

I wondered if she knew Betts.

Her fingers began to tremble. Her waxen-skin palm bypassed Travis's outstretched hand and moved toward the eye of Horus charm I wore around my neck. She rubbed her thumb over the engraving and chanted words I'd heard before: "Ocha kiniba nita ochun—cheke cheke cheke."

Travis slid his arm in mine and tugged.

Mrs. Curtis motioned for me to wait. Digging beneath the folds of her skirt, she fished out a watery-pink crystal. Raising it slowly, she mumbled below her breath and pressed it between my eyes. "A gift of healing."

Stepping back, I assured her, "I'm perfectly healthy."

She closed the space between us and dropped the crystal into my jacket pocket. Her lips pressed into my ear. "I foresee a time when this rose quartz will heal a wounded heart."

Unraveling a five, I offered it to her. She refused the money and disappeared in the crowd.

"Let me see that," Travis said.

I handed him the weighty, faceted, nonprecious stone. It had a silver clasp affixed to the tip in case you wanted to wear it on a chain. He rolled it in his palm. "It's a setup. This psychic thing is about scamming people's emotions for profit."

The angular crystal was smooth to the touch. For safekeeping, I slipped it back into my pocket. "Mrs. Curtis is Trudy's neighbor. She lives alone, probably doesn't have family around." I swirled my fingers near my temples. "She's the type that fuels herself with paranoia."

We walked over purple carpet with exploding firework burst designs. I didn't need to smoke in here. In an arena as large as a football field, my head buzzed with patchouli-fortified air. Like a mega grocery store, a maze of aisles was filled with booths that peddled services and products to sort out the esoteric you. We passed healers and hecklers who offered flower and teacup readings, guardian angel advice, chakra balancing, five-minute connections to ancestral spirits, and a gazillion other on-the-spot services costing from five to fifty dollars.

"This place is rip-off central, and you've been targeted."

"It was just an old lady screwing around. She probably goes home and has a howl after she freaks people out with her crazy chant."

Travis dropped my arm and clenched my shoulders. "Admit it. You attract the unstable type, and inside a psychic expo you're outnumbered. I don't think it's a brilliant idea to snoop around."

"The last thing I'm going to do is provoke any of these clairvoyant mystic types." I locked my arm in his. "Now let's find out what Betts's hold is on my mother."

Opening a trifold brochure, Travis asked, "What's Betts's specialty? Tarot cards, teacup readings, levitation?"

"Those are just her hobbies. Her forte is aura reading, clearing, and repair."

"What the hell is that?"

"She looks at spiritual energy. The colors that encircle you. She says she can help clients get in touch with their energy, cut negative cords, and release blocks."

"Sounds like a brain enema."

My feet locked in front of a booth that looked like an old-fashioned candy store. But instead of sweets, dried flower heads, mixed herbs, and powders filled glass jars. A side table held dozens of Easter baskets filled with colorfully labeled oil vials.

A twentysomething guy wearing a black silk shirt and a red sash tied around his waist swept a silver-handled scoop over the containers. He addressed us in a twangy accent. "Perhaps a love potion?"

Travis pretended his curiosity wasn't piqued.

I liked the view in front of me, and my imagination became lost in the silky black folds that cascaded down his buff chest. I decided he had to be a descendent of Don Diego de la Vega—a.k.a. Zorro. Only this hot hombre peddled herbal potions.

Zorro held a cheesecloth sash the size of my palm. Opening it, he scooped raspberry-colored freeze-dried rose heads for a waiting customer. Curling his index finger, he beckoned me closer. A heavy musk traveled from his neck to my nose. In a syrupy drawl, he said, "Maybe some lemon verbena. It will cause a rift between lovers, leaving my door of opportunity open."

Did he hit on all the women that came through? *Probably*. I pinched my smile. "You don't look like you need herbal potions to find romance."

Zorro raised his eyebrows.

Travis lost interest. He snatched my wrist and pulled me away. "Come on, Rachael."

"Travis," I huffed.

He stopped a few booths away. "For real? A southern gypsy dressed in a black silk shirt, who sells herbs and oils. What are you thinking?"

"He's hot. And don't try and tell me you think he's gay."

"I was not attracted to him, so you don't have to worry about battling me for his affections."

His strong arm led me around a corner. As I pulled free of his grip, Travis and I gawked at Betts's Aura Guidance booth, where Mom was placing a handful of pamphlets in a plastic bag before using a credit card imprinter on some stranger's card. Her Dorothy Hamel haircut had grown out, and gray roots bled into her straight-edged brunette cut. If her hairstyle had been the only change, I could have dealt. But her growing roots swallowed up the Mom I knew. The one who was there for me unconditionally. After time away at school, I'd thought I could handle this new passion of hers. It was easier when she practiced being psychic in Arizona. Whatever had budded inside of her was foreign to me. Since she'd come back to Canton, being in the same room made me uncomfortable, and until now, I realized I'd avoided her.

A center table, partially shielded with curtains, rested on a raised platform. Betts sat across from a wide-eyed stranger, who, I assumed, had paid her to shovel her spiel. The air-conditioning inside the expo would have kept fresh meat from spoiling, but watching her, a molten anger bubbled inside of me. My emotions were tired of being buried. I knew I had to clear the air and talk to Mom. "Come on," I told Travis.

"Rachael, Travis," my mom said.

I gave her a hug. "Hi, Mom."

To give me some alone-time, and not wanting anything to do with an intervention, Travis began flipping through the assortment of books and pamphlets for sale. He let out an open-mouthed gawk when he spotted *The Ten Meditative Steps to Maintaining An Erection.*

"So what do you do here all day?" I asked.

Mom picked up some books that had been left on a table and organized them into the shelves. "I restock and handle all the appointments."

"Do you do readings?"

"No, not yet. I'm still apprenticing."

I ran my finger down the page of the schedule that lay open. There were five names penciled in for the entire day. "And you're able to make a living doing this?"

Snapping the book closed, she said, "Betts is a highly acclaimed aura reader. She has a following. People travel—"

"What are you doing?"

She motioned her hands upward. "I'm working."

Softening my voice, I asked, "Are you being blackmailed for something? What is Betts's holding over you?"

She bit her lip and blinked. "Someone paying some attention to me, to my higher self, makes me happy."

My voice defied me, and words came out louder and sharper than I meant. "You have dark circles under your eyes, you've gained weight, and you've barely said two words to me or Dad since you've been in town. You've given up the things you loved. Your identity."

"Rachael, you have no right to come here and say hurtful things to me. I'm your mother."

"You hung up that hat when you took off without an explanation. In nine months, you only called me twice."

Like a steam train, I barreled down the tracks and blurted out the emotional baggage that my mom's abrupt departure had strapped on my back. I was so focused on launching my words that I didn't see the tall, spiky-haired figure move toward me.

Betts spoke in a French accent. "Le circlip de missy." *Listen here, missy?* Grabbing her own hand, she spoke again. This time without an accent, "Cherise, no, don't do it."

Mom drew her hand over her mouth.

"Listen, Cherise Betts, or whoever you really are. You've done enough with your relationship wrecking ball. This conversation is none of your business."

Betts slapped me across my cheek, derailing my diatribe.

Apparently she didn't appreciate my words of wisdom.

My head snapped back, and my ears went bionic, honing in on the pulsing of my beating heart. It took me a moment to register what had happened. A searing sting pulsed. *Betts had walloped my face.*

Jumping in front of me, Travis shouted, "That was out of line!"

I tasted blood. There was a scuffle. My motor skills were on pause. My vision seemed fuzzy. Was I really seeing a woman in spandex tip over a chair to get at Betts? "Trudy?"

Travis pulled me backward. "Watch out."

From the middle of the booth, a customer scrambled to make a hasty exit. I peered around Travis and watched Trudy wrap a toned forearm around Betts's neck. Mom grabbed Trudy's waist, and the three of them tumbled toward the table where Betts had been giving a session.

From under the free-for-all of shouts and grunts, Betts called out "Hector," and a man from behind the back curtain came forward.

Stunned from the sting on my face, I forgot to breathe. A rapid fire of hiccups erupted out of me. Pressing his car keys in my hand, Travis barked orders. "Go to my car. I'll meet you there."

As I moved away, I glanced over my shoulder. Hector and Travis were working at pulling the yarn ball of bodies apart. The struggle escalated into a yelling match, and I watched Trudy trap Betts's legs between her thighs. Everyone was focused on the wrestling match. No one noticed me as I slipped behind the curtain to the back of the booth. At best, I had a minute to snoop.

Towers of cardboard boxes were stacked in the back corner. I opened one up. Newspapers padded spirit guidebooks and tarot card sets. Voices I didn't recognize erupted on the other side of the curtain. I peeked out and heard Trudy accuse my mom of abandonment. I shut the drape when Mom called Trudy a gold digger.

Trudy was a lot of things, but gold digger didn't fit in the descriptive I'd use to peg her.

With stealth speed, I opened two more boxes. *What am I doing?* Dropping to my knees, I felt fatigued. Last time I checked, selling books and tarot cards was not illegal. Ink stained my hands, and I unfolded the balled-up newspaper I'd grasped from a box. *The Colorado Springs Daily* local section. The date on the top right was May 18, 1987. Two months ago. Mechanically I opened another box. More books. I uncrumpled another newspaper. *The Wichita Eagle*, Feb 4, 1987. I felt desperate. Regardless of whether or not Mom and Dad got back together, I wanted Betts out of my family's life. How could I make that happen? All I'd found was a bunch of newspapers from different cities. *So what?*

A voice beyond the fabric divider boomed, "Break it up, ladies."

I peeped out through a crack. Security had arrived.

Trudy asked Travis, "Where's Rachael?"

"She went to my car."

Reality drew a fat tear in the corner of my eye. I was the head case. Why did I want to change my mother? She'd made her wishes clear. A hiccup snuck up my throat. My mother's mentor had decked me, and the only defense Mom had offered was a startled face. Struggling against the sting of rejection, I inhaled my emotions. I needed to get a grip, but my gut wouldn't let me. It kept telling me that there was more than aura readings to Betts. If I couldn't talk my mom out of leaving her, I needed a new plan, one that would put the head nuts-o somewhere inaccessible.

My eyes readjusted to the dim light behind the booth. Under a card table was a macramé purse with a leather handle. Reaching my hand into the center pocket, I fanned my fingers past an expo pamphlet, a hairbrush, and a cosmetic case. On the bottom, next to a half-empty whisky pint, was a plastic bag filled with yellow powder that looked like dried mustard. In a side compartment, I found a pocket-sized memo pad and pulled it out for closer inspection. Names and addresses were listed with scribbled notations. *Dedra Gray, husband deceased, Forest Park, gated.* Below it was another notation. *Pierce Simmers, Fox Run, travels first and third week.* Were these clients? If she were a real aura reader, she wouldn't have to do homework before she had an appointment. I took a deep breath, blanked my mind, and flipped through the pages.

Footsteps scampered nearby. I didn't want to be found. Dropping the notebook back into the purse, I crawled under a curtain divider to the next booth.

NOTE TO SELF
A black silk shirt is not cheesy when it's worn by a hot Zorro.

My gut was right about Betts. She has a bad aura and a wicked hand.

8

Allegorical Guise

Outside of the expo center, I took three deep breaths and tried to smother the haze in my head. Afternoon storms had swept their gray clouds east, leaving a clear ink sky. I didn't know how long it would take Travis to meet me, but I hoped he'd be quick. My emotions tottered between hurt and anger. I needed to get away from here and organize my head.

Psychics and healers weren't immune to addictions. Gathered in corners near the double-door side entrance, exotic women standing in a huddle blew smoke as they shared their encounters with unreasonable client demands.

"I just read what I see, I can't manipulate it," a woman in a purple-feather-trimmed jacket vented.

From the inside pocket of my denim jacket, I tapped out a cigarette. Tucking the wafer-thin paper between my lips, I plunked down on a bench between giant pebbled concrete pots. The maple trees that grew inside the planters canopied the concrete below. Seated next to a lush forest, I dipped my head between my knees and massaged my fingers into my temples.

Funny thing about cigarettes. Pressing one between my lips provided clarity. *Coming here was a dumb idea.* What was I thinking? That Betts would slip up—admit that she was a con—in front of my mom? That Mom would realize how wrong she'd been to have left? The inner me put her hands on her hips and tapped her foot. *Yeah, that's exactly what you thought.*

Today had only proven how distant Mom had become. Her psychic quest left little room for those from her past. Physically she was the woman who gave birth to me, but inside...Hell, I didn't know who she was anymore, and now I wasn't so sure I wanted to find out.

Sitting upright, I toyed my fingers through the silk scarf tied to my head. From behind, someone flicked a lighter and placed it near my face. The flame startled me, and the unlit cigarette dropped out of my mouth. "Zorro?"

"My name's not Zorro. It's Lightnin' Horse."

I choked, "Seriously?"

"No," he drawled. "This bench taken?"

Motioning with my open hand, I retrieved my cigarette from the ground. "You're from the South?"

Zorro left half a body space between us and stretched his tanned arms across the bench back. I noticed a chunky wristwatch, black with lots of dials. He reached his right hand to mine. "Jackson Kimball."

His strong fingers encased mine longer than appropriate for a friendly introduction. "Rachael O'Brien," I said, not feeling particularly chatty.

Jackson held his gaze on my face. His attention made me squirm, and I looked over my shoulder for Travis.

"You all right? I don't mean to sound rude, but you've got a plum swellin' on your cheek."

I winced. "Yeah. I had an altercation with my mom's spiritual healer."

He reached into a hidden pocket beneath his shirt folds and pulled out several plastic tubes. They reminded me of the perfume and lipstick samples that the door-to-door Avon lady left behind. Sorting them in his palm, he asked, "What happened?"

"It's complicated."

Selecting a tube with clear liquid, he said, "Anything worthwhile is. May I?"

Nervously I twitched my cigarette ash into a carpet of geraniums that grew in the planter next to me. "What is that?"

He tipped a drop of the oil onto his index finger. "Lavender. It'll help heal the bruisin.'" Placing his free hand on my forehead, he tilted my head back and ran his fingers around the crown of my head to the base of my neck, then delicately dabbed a drop onto my cheek. I didn't know this guy, but his touch made my stomach flip-flop.

Handing me the vial, he said, "Put a little on before you go to bed and in the morning."

I stroked my cheek. "Thanks."

Dragging two fingers across my eyebrow, he pushed some strands of hair to my temple. "How exactly did you enrage a spiritual healer?"

This guy's company replaced my self-pity with lusty visions. My pride blew her whistle. *Should you share this drama with a stranger?*

This herbal healer was taking me for a Sunday drive, directionless but highly therapeutic, and I kicked my pesky conscience aside. Tucking my knees under my arms, I rattled, "Last fall, two weeks into my freshman term at North Carolina College, Mom left my dad to find her planetary psychic self. We've barely heard from her, until now. She just showed up with her head healer. They have a booth inside. I confronted my mom."

Diffused lamplights cast a soft glow around Jackson, his defined jaw, smooth neck, and broad shoulders. "What did you say to her?"

He was attentive, hanging on my words, so I continued. "When I asked my mom what was she doing with her life, her watchdog smacked me."

Jackson's mouth gaped. He sat up. "Who's the watchdog?"

"Betts. I don't know her last name."

"Betsy McMurtie? Stocky woman, wears lots of jangly jewelry, fascination with mythical spiritualism?"

"You know her?"

"Aura healer. Yeah. She buys from me. Wait a minute. Are you Maeve's daughter?"

"Ya," I stuttered.

Taken aback, Jackson said, "Your mom is sweet. She told me all about you."

This was the guy Betts had mentioned the night we ate pot roast, after the picnic table went up in flames. "What exactly did she say?"

Jackson's lips curled into a smile. "That you were a freshman at North Carolina College, studying art history."

"That's all she said?"

His eyes locked with mine, sending an electric volt that stood my arm hairs on edge. "Is there more I should know?"

"So what exactly does Betts buy from you?"

"Herbs and oils. Cleared me out of African ginger."

I scrunched my nose. Mom's cooking spanned all ethnicities, Vietnamese, Indian, Moroccan, but I'd never seen African ginger in her spice rack. "What?"

Hunching forward, he rested his elbows on his knees and pondered the night. I followed his stare toward the parking lot. I didn't see anything. Just a couple of guys unloading boxes off a van. "Generally it's used as a natural anti-inflammatory and circulatory stimulant."

Natural anti-inflammatory, circulatory stimulant? Was Zorro for real or just another practiced schmoozer?

"A cure for indigestion, nausea, gas, and congestion. Although some people use it for its magical qualities."

Here we go. I knew he was too cute to be normal.

Jackson's thumb stroked my unblemished cheek. "It's said to ward off trouble and provide protection. Sometimes it's used in spells for love and money."

His caramel-coated drawl lured me toward him. God, I had to get a grip. I didn't even know this guy.

"You've got to be kidding."

He shook his head. "African ginger is a plant with large, hairless leaves. The root is harvested. I sell it in powder form."

"What color is it?"

"Yellow. The shade varies dependin' on the region and growin' conditions. The smell is pungent, the taste hot, biting. With all its medical uses, the plant demand can't be sustained. There are import-export regulations. I have a hard time keeping it in stock."

"How do you know all this?"

"It's my business. Herbal-U. I have a BS in biology and nutrition from Tulane."

My eyes widened at the mention of the Bayou region.

"Have you ever been to Louisiana?"

Dragging my tongue across my eyetooth, I said, "Once." But didn't delve into any particulars regarding my New Orleans experience. "You conduct business at psychic expos?"

Leaning back, his hips closed the space between us, and he curled his arm around my shoulder.

Is he hitting on me?

"Just the larger industry shows. I meet my target consumers, do some research on trends, and make wholesale contacts." He brushed the tails of my scarf behind my shoulder and leaned in. His breath tickled my neck. "And it seems I've even met the girl who—"

"Rach!" Travis shouted from behind.

AFTER A COMPLETE ANALYSIS in the car, Travis and I had determined that Betts was a control freak. More disturbing, she seemed obsessed with my mother, whom she wanted to keep as a love slave. And my presence threatened everything Betts had worked so hard to secure. What we couldn't figure out was why come to Canton? Was the expo worth the risk of reuniting Mom with Dad and me?

Travis parked his Volvo in a guest parking spot outside of Trudy's apartment building. She must have left the expo around the same time we did. Her Volkswagen Cabriolet was three spots down. Dad's annoying girlfriend sticking up for me had tipped the balance inside my emotional cauldron. I'd convinced myself that she was a nuisance, but today she had my back and tangled with Betts.

"Stop laughing," I said.

"About what?" he giggled.

"Getting slapped isn't funny."

"Sorry. I just can't get the pileup of bodies in the booth out of my head. It was so Roller Derby-ish"

"Jeez, I'm glad I have a friend who is so sensitive to my feelings."

"It was like the Three Stooges in there."

"Slapping me was stupid. I can't believe Trudy, not my mom, lashed out at Betts. Isn't protection supposed to be wired into mothers?"

"Rach, she was in as much shock as the rest of us."

"Did she ask where I went?"

Travis slid his arm around my shoulder and squeezed before he shook his head.

Had she ever even loved me?

"After you left, it was weird."

Weirder?

"Your mom was mostly embarrassed with the unwanted attention drawn to the booth. She seemed worried that Betts was mad at something."

"Maybe I'm adopted," I said, warming to the idea. Then I remembered I'd seen dozens of preggo and newborn photo moments in my baby album.

Travis fetched his overnight bag from the trunk. Stars had emerged in the clear night sky, and moonlight reflected off the man-made pond where crickets and frogs collided in a fiesta of chirps and croaks. I slapped the tender skin behind my knee too late. A bug bite began to swell.

Outside Trudy's apartment, I peered behind the bushes near the lamppost.

Travis tapped me on my shoulder. "Expecting someone?"

"We should go up and get you settled into Trudy's apartment."

"I'm not sure she's back," he said. "Security made her leave the booth. They threatened to detain her, and she looked frazzled."

"Her car is here. She's back."

Travis wrapped his arm around my shoulder and guided me up the stairs to the entrance of the building. "Did you give Zorro your number?"

Rubbing my tongue over my eyetooth, I decided how to respond.

Releasing my shoulder, he said, "You naughty trollop. Have you arranged to see him?"

"I have a hypothetical question. If Zorro had kissed me, and if I kissed him back, would that have been like cheating on Clay?"

"Are you telling me that in the ten minutes I left you alone, you managed to work your Rachael magic and engage in a make out session?"

"No," my voice squeaked. "This is hypothetical."

Travis tapped me on the tip of my nose. "Technically you and Clay aren't speaking."

I pushed his hand off my face. "But I've been lusting after him for almost a year. If Clay is the one, I shouldn't be interested in anyone else, right?"

"You don't have an exclusivity agreement. You're free to lock lips with whomever you please. So when are you seeing Zorro?"

"He didn't ask me out on a date. He just penned his number on a scrap of paper."

Travis nudged my arm. "Call him. It could be considered practice."

Climbing the staircase to Trudy's apartment, a flash of panic ignited. Sky and I hadn't cleaned up after we'd slept over. Trudy would freak if she thought someone spent the night—which someone had. *I'd have to fess up, otherwise she'd never move out of our house.*

Trudy's apartment door stood ajar; her keys hung from the door lock. I knuckle knocked. "Hey, Trudy."

Even outside the gym, she wore a fitted spandex bodysuit under a sleeveless torn-neck sweat shirt. I watched the muscles in her forearms tighten as she rotated in a circle. I had a sinking feeling. *She knew someone had stayed here.*

Stepping beyond her foyer, I covered a gasp. Someone had cleaned since Sky and I had stayed here. "Your apartment is so—tidy."

"It's worse than I remember," she burbled.

"What are you talking about?" Travis asked.

Seeing me, Trudy switched her facial contortions from shock to horror. "Oh, Rachael. Your face—it's swollen." She guided me into a corner of her living room and twisted the knob of a halogen lamp to get a closer look. "We need to call your father."

"Does he know you were at the expo?"

Trudy looked toward the kitchen. "No."

"Why were you there?"

"Mostly curiosity."

"About my mom?"

She nodded.

"I'm not telling Dad, and neither are you."

Unwilling to referee this one, Travis plopped into a butterfly chair.

Trudy's mouth flexed downward, and she made puppy eyes. "Betts is living under your father's roof and has assaulted you in front of your mother. This isn't some little thing you can keep from him."

"I'll tell him, just not tonight. The Fourth of July is tomorrow. Travis is only here two more nights. I just want to wait until the holiday is over."

This was the highest word count I'd ever spoken to Trudy.

She crossed her arms and pondered my request.

Travis took it all in. I could tell he knew I was up to something. I didn't mention the loose plan that involved snooping, and if Dad kicked Mom and Betts out of the apartment, I'd be back at square one. I needed time to check on a few things.

"Please, Trudy. Just stay quiet for a day. I'll tell Dad when Travis leaves."

She uncrossed her arms. "I want your word that you'll tell him on Monday."

"I promise."

"And."

"And what?"

"I want you to start coming to step aerobics three times a week to strengthen your calf and dodgy shoulder. Starting tomorrow."

"That's blackmail."

She smiled.

Trudy handed Travis her apartment key and moved to turn on a hall-way light. "Help yourself to the refrigerator."

"Sorry you can't stay at the house, but it's at capacity," I said loudly. Lowering my voice, I leaned toward Travis's ear. "Dad would die before he let you sleep in my bedroom, and I'd die if I had to share it with Trudy."

"Don't worry about me."

"Make sure you lock the door behind us," I said.

"Definitely."

Trudy and I made it to her car without bumping into Mrs. Curtis or Doneski, which was a bonus.

"Wanna drive home with the top down?"

"Really," I said, secretly stoked. I so loved her car.

TRUDY SLOWED DOWN AT a yellow light and stopped as it turned red. I had fifteen miles of close quarters with her until we got home. Her Volkswagen Cabriolet was the only car at the intersection, and I so wanted her to gun through the light. I was anxious to get home and into my room without Dad seeing my face.

"Travis is a good guy," Trudy said. "He talked security into letting me go."

"He didn't tell me that. What did Betts and my mom have to say for themselves?"

"Were you there when I had Betts pinned between my knees?"

"Yeah, I saw it. Did Aunt G teach you that?"

Trudy smiled. "I should've guessed Aunt G wrestles. I haven't had the pleasure of a lesson from her."

The light turned green, and as Trudy accelerated, warm summer air fanned my face.

"Betts went all limp like, shut her eyes, and then popped them open. I thought she was having an asthma attack or something, so I released my leg grip."

"Trudy, she was faking it."

"I'm not so sure. I mean, her eye rolling, going all stiff seemed so bizarre. Even her cheeks lost their color. How could anyone turn that on so quickly?"

"She's a con. She probably started this crap as a kid, when she didn't get her way. I'm guessing she's had years of acting experience. How did you leave things?"

"When I left with a security escort, Betts went into a spasm. Her breath became erratic, and her face grew pink blotchy patches. She started telling some sort of prophecy in a really weird, deep voice."

I scoffed. "Like what? 'The world is going to end unless you donate a massive sum to Betts's aura reading?'"

Trudy bit her cheek.

"What did she say?"

Trudy sighed. "I think she cursed me."

"Did she call you a shithead or something?"

"Not a swear curse, a real one."

Pressing her lips tight, she concentrated on the road.

"Come on, Trudy. What are you afraid of?"

"That it'll come true. She told your mom and security that an unwanted spirit entered her. And it, not her, slapped you."

My blood simmered. "You're shittin' me?" *She is completely mental.*

"Your mom believed her. Told security she's seen it before. When Betts does too many readings, her defenses weaken, and spirits are able to enter her aura."

"Betts's brain wiring is fried. Thanks for being there," I said, not believing that I was grateful for Dad's girlfriend. The one I thought was a complete airhead. At the moment she seemed to care about me more than Mom.

The streets were quiet, and only a few cars passed us on the winding road. Trudy shifted into third gear and gnawed her lip.

"Is there anything else?" I asked.

She tilted her back, and I was worried that she'd crash into something. "What is it?"

"Betts said you and I are in danger, and that it's no use running from our destiny."

NOTE TO SELF

Does inhaling patchouli strengthen opposing personality tolerances? Not feeling as annoyed with Trudy and not sure why!

9

High Highs and Low Lows

Travis motored us along a country road surrounded by fields of corn. The leafy stalks stood seven feet tall with ears growing on the tips. Wind swayed the hairy tassels that grew out of the husks. I'd barely slept. Now, in addition to the bruise on my cheek, I had dark circles under my eyes. I'd applied layers of powder and foundation. Flipping Travis's car mirror visor up, I asked, "Can you see a bruise?"

He dropped his sunglasses, and I tilted my head. "How'd you hide it?"

"Liquid concealer. Take a right."

"Isn't this the street your dad's shop is on? I thought we were going to Gert's?"

"I just need to check on something."

Travis pulled into the gravel driveway. "What do you need to check on? It's the Fourth of July."

The parking lot was empty. I glanced at the second-story window and swatted Travis's shoulder. "When's the last time you climbed a tree?"

"No, forget it. I'm not breaking in."

"My dad owns the building, so technically it's not breaking in. Besides, we're not going into the shop, we're going into the apartment above."

Travis rolled his window down and cut the car engine.

"Rachael, this is stupid. What do you expect to find in there?"

I slumped my head back and spoke to the upholstered car roof. "I don't know. Probably nothing. But maybe something."

"What kind of something?"

"Something to convince my mother she's better off without Betts. I don't care if Mom thinks she's psychic or wants to practice hocus-pocus. I just want her to do it in Canton, without Betts."

Travis tsked and shook his head.

I got out of the car and slammed the door. Walking to the driver's side, I bent my elbows on the open window. "Are you coming, or am I climbing the buckeye alone?"

He frowned. "Let's get this over with. Gert promised to show me how to shoot twenty-one monkey."

"Twenty-one monkey?" I repeated. Aunt G had to be farfing around with Travis. I'd never seen a pool shot called monkey.

Travis fitted his hands together, and I plunged my foot into his hand lock. His fingers pulled apart, landing me on my ass. "You did that on purpose."

He made a meager effort to suppress a laugh. "I did not."

"Squat down," I said.

"Why?"

"So I can climb onto your shoulders."

Travis wobbled toward a sturdy branch that met my chest. Scrambling aboard, I asked, "Are you coming?"

He jumped, but his fingertips couldn't grasp the branch. "I'll be the lookout."

As I clambered up the tree, Travis fired useless commentary. "Not that branch. Careful, O'Brien. If you fall, you're going to seriously break something."

I could see the double-pane window. It was on a swing hinge and hung open. Locusts hummed in the wild browned grass clumps that grew near a vacant building behind the restoration shop.

Travis's chin tilted up, and he raised a hand against the afternoon sun. Since it was a holiday, local businesses were closed. Without car or foot traffic, the neighboring parking lots were empty. The eerie quiet ignited paranoia. Spying was an intrusion of privacy. What can I say? We all have vices, and I happen to be more of the discovery type. I filed the activity under "Thwarting bad behavior with bad behavior."

Shimmying across a limb, I realized cotton Bermuda shorts were not the best wardrobe choice. In direct route to the apartment window, I nicked and scraped the inside of my bare legs.

"That branch doesn't look strong enough," Travis warned.

Plush green finger leaves rattled under a breeze. I hadn't been above the workshop in years. Edmond used to live up here, but he had moved out when he found a fixer-upper with a barn out back to restore his Airstream. By then, Dad's business had picked up, and he had decided not to rent out the space. With high-priced art being restored below, Dad was careful. The apartment was now only used for an occasional out-of-town visitor.

The buckeye tree towered over the building and provided shade from the direct sunlight. As a kid, I'd fired the glossy nuts from a slingshot at a boy whose dad worked at one of the neighboring businesses. My aim has always been precise, and at close range, I'd nailed my opponent on the base of his neck. He grew a raspberry welt the size of a half-dollar coin. I had to apologize, and Dad had confiscated my weaponry, which put a damper on future attacks.

The branch I climbed across intertwined with others. Even though there were no cars besides ours in the lot, a rush of adrenaline pumped. Within an arm's reach of the open window, I peered into the loft to make sure it was empty. Through the mesh screen I could see the Amish quilts on the beds. Ceiling beams were exposed, and honey wood paneling covered the walls. Mom had left an oscillating fan running on top of the corner dresser. The double beds took up most of the space. There was a compact kitchen with a minifridge and stove top in the far corner. Three doors were closed. One opened to an outer staircase that landed out back. The second door, locked from the other side, was a spiral staircase that dropped into a corner of the shop. The third door hid an airplane-sized bathroom with sink and standing shower.

I recognized Mom's side of the room instantly. Not by the clothes or personal items, but by how she kept them. Her things were stacked and perfectly folded with square corners. The closer side was kept less anal with clothes escaping the unclosed zipper of an overpacked suitcase.

The screen easily popped, and I pushed inside.

"Careful," Travis warned.

Straddling the windowsill, I plunked into the bedroom without grace, and as I thumped to the floor, I mangled the screen. "Shit."

"What happened?"

I hung my head out the window and dangled the V-shaped framed mesh. "The screen is kind of bent."

"The metal should be soft. Try to straighten it on your knee."

Sitting on a bed I plied it back into a rectangle-ish shape. Eyeing Betts's stuff, I pegged her as a jewelry hoarder. A velvet carrier lay un-rolled on the floor, and jangly Victorian-looking pieces poked out. A necklace and matching earrings with cabochon sapphires and pearls en-crusted in diamonds. For someone who professed knowledge rather than material goods as an aspiration, she sure had a lot of expensive-looking accessories. I kicked her suitcase lid open with my foot. Closing my eyes, I plunged my hands in. Like wading your feet on the murky ocean floor for sand dollars, my hands were in blind territory, and an unwanted vi-sual of touching her panties made me shudder. On the bottom, I felt a folder and tugged.

"Rach, hurry up," Travis shouted.

I leaned out the window. "Just a few more minutes."

The file tab sticker read *Geneva McCarty. Betts had stolen the client folder from Dad's desk. But why?*

Popping a window screen out is easy. Putting it back while straddling a tree branch, not as simple. I'd tucked Geneva's folder down the butt of my shorts. Ignoring the rough paper on skin sensation, I struggled to fit the bent screen back in place.

A warm breeze fluttered the supple finger leaves, tapping them against one another in a fairy song. Scooting forward, I leaned toward the screen and intended to use brute force.

"Try to secure the corners in the channel brackets."

"Why don't we switch places?" I smarted off.

The branch beneath me groaned, and I became hyperaware of holding still. Lifting the screen in place, I jammed my palm against it and heard a snap under my thighs. The fall lurched me forward until I faceplanted into dirt. The drop to the ground knocked the wind from my chest, and as my lungs constricted, I lay motionless.

Some smartass crow voiced a series of caws from the tree canopy, and I heard Travis's shoes shuffle across the gravel. He flipped me onto my back. "Rachael, can you hear me?"

I sucked wind and groaned. "How could I not hear you? You're screaming in my face."

He pulled a leafy branch with green buckeyes still attached from my hair. Grass blade tips that had gone to seed and turned brown irritated the soft skin beneath my knees. After a minute, I rolled onto my side and sat up.

"Is anything broken?" he asked.

After smoothing my hair back and reaffixing my ponytail, I patted my bum shoulder. "Still in one piece."

"What about your leg?"

I bent and flexed it. "Still working."

Travis helped me stand. We settled into the Adirondack chairs, and I inspected the cuts and scrapes on my arms and legs.

"Let's just get out of here. I told you, Betts wouldn't be stupid enough to leave anything incriminating up there."

I reached down the backside of my shorts.

"What the crap is that?"

"This is a client file from my dad's desk. I found it in her suitcase. She's using my mother."

"Are you sure? There could be a reasonable explanation."

I shook my head. "She's working an angle."

"What angle? What does a client file provide to Betts?"

Betts was a fool to come to Canton. What did she think, that she'd screw with Dad and my life a little more? Did she think that since she had Mom on her side, she could pick us off next? "I'm not sure what her plan is, but I'm onto her, and I'm having a premonition that her veil of hocus-pocus will soon be lifted."

NOTE TO SELF
May have touched Betts's underpants in my reconnaissance operation. Grody!

Climbing trees is not as much fun as I remember. Recovering from bumpy buckeye landing, branch bruises, and a deep paperesque laceration on my ass.

I am onto Betts. Can't wait to chew her up and spit her out. The spit out portion will blow her aura.

10

Vanished Under a Kaboom

Italian-style Fourth of July was a new tradition, thanks to Trudy. Instead of hot dogs, hamburgers, and potato salad, my dad, Travis, Gert, Sky, and I gorged on antipasti salad, lasagna, Italian sausage, peppers, onions, and assorted mini cheesecakes for dessert. It was takeout, and way better than the last fondue Thanksgiving Trudy had hosted. I was actually okay with it.

Travis and I met Dad, Trudy, and Sky at Aunt G's. Dad didn't know about my altercation with Betts, and I wasn't sure if he or Aunt G had invited Mom and *her*. If they'd been invited, I wasn't sure they'd show.

Trudy went all out arranging platters of meatball and calamari appetizers with mini flag toothpicks. Gert rounded up Travis, Sky, and me for a game of twenty-one monkey. I half listened to her rules. "One cue ball in the pocket—orders a drink. Seven in the pocket tastes the drink. Fourteen drinks the drink. Last ball in pays for the round unless the person who sunk fourteen hasn't finished. Then they pay." She sounded convincing, but I'd known Gert all my life, and I'd never played twenty-one monkeys. I was sure she'd made up the game on the spot.

"But we're not in a bar," Sky said.

Aunt Gert selected her cue. "We'll improvise."

"Why's it called 'twenty-one monkey'?" Travis asked.

Chalking her cue stick, she confessed, "Because that's the most rounds I've played in a single night."

"Tonight may be a record breaker," Travis teased.

Leaving caution behind, I sipped a strawberry daiquiri with blueberry whipped topping, a holiday cocktail that Trudy had handed me. I asked her if it was healthy, and she assured me it was not.

Resting my back against the wood-paneled wall, I watched Trudy and Dad slip outside. I liked how the walls that Dad had sanded and stained felt against my skin. They were sturdy and polished, the way my life used to be.

Sky nudged me. "Are you okay?"

Outside Gert's picture window, I could see Dad seated in a chaise lounge next to Trudy. He laughed as she fed him something drippy off a toothpick. I couldn't remember ever seeing him happy like that. *Could I be wrong about Trudy?*

"I'm great," I said, completely lying. "You know that night we spent at Trudy's?"

"Yeah?"

"Did you come back later and spot clean her place?"

"I completely forgot. Did Trudy say something?"

"No. No one said anything. It's just that Travis has been staying there, and it's way cleaner than we left it."

Sky contorted her face. "Are you sure? Who could get in there, and why would they want to?"

"Your shot," Gert called to Sky.

What was going on? Doneski? No. He's a creep, but not a neat freak.

Travis caught my eye, and I smiled at him. It was good to have his company, and I'd miss him when he left. He'd helped me out of the expo center and scooped my flattened ass out from under the buckeye tree. I wouldn't subject him to Dad's ballistic reaction and planned to wait until tomorrow after he left to fess up about Betts and what I found.

From outside, Dad shouted my name in a nonfestive tone. His call was the kind that draws creases into his forehead. It was the tone he used when I was in trouble. At the front door, he gripped my arm and tugged me outside, causing daiquiri to slosh out of my glass. Standing a few feet behind him, Trudy bit her lip as she analyzed her strappy sandals.

Making squinty snake eyes at the girlfriend, I had an inkling what had upset my dad. Under a flat smile, I mouthed, "Thanks."

When Trudy's head surfaced, she whispered, "Sorry."

Dad lifted his sunglasses onto his head and squinted at my cheek. "Why didn't you tell me?"

"Tell you what?"

"I'm not playing that game."

"What game?"

While pacing, he ran his fingers through his hair. "Rachael, your mother and Betts assaulted you, and you didn't tell me."

"Technically the slap was battery. And Mom didn't launch it, Betts did when she allowed some demented spirit from a client to enter her weakened aura."

His legs locked, and his face went all glazed donut. For a moment, I wondered if he'd become possessed.

"My God, Rachael, her behavior is not normal."

"Agreed."

Dad wrapped me in his arms and kissed my forehead. "You need to tell me about these things when they happen."

"I didn't tell you because I didn't want to lose her again. Betts is the problem, not Mom."

"Your mother has taken us both on an emotional roller coaster. I've played nice, letting her and that woman stay above the shop. I hoped that she would repair some of the damage, at least between you two." Dad held me by my shoulders. "But I will not tolerate violence."

His voice sounded so raw. I decided to fess up about my entry-with-out-permission discovery. "Promise you won't be mad at me if I tell you something important?"

"What?"

"Promise."

"Rachael, I promise."

"I kind of climbed the buckeye when Mom and Betts weren't in the apartment and kind of found Geneva McCarty's client file in the bottom of Betts's suitcase, and I kind of took it."

Red blotches crept up his neck and onto his cheeks. "When was this?"

"Just before lunch."

"Were you alone?"

"No, Travis was with me."

"Where's the folder?"

I pointed toward the car. "In the glove box."

"Go get it."

"You promised you wouldn't be mad."

"I promised not to be mad at you, and I'm not. I am mad as hell at your irresponsible mother and her sidekick."

"What are you going to do?"

"Get Travis. I want you two to come along. Betts is no longer welcome under my roof."

"But if you kick Betts out, Mom will leave."

BEFORE THE NIGHT TURNED DARK, random rocket blasts popped off in backyards. Charcoaled-hot-dog-scented air blew into the open window. From the backseat of Dad's two-door vintage truck, I leaned forward.

It was the Fourth of July, and all of normal America was at a picnic waiting for the fireworks show. But my family was no longer normal. As much as I struggled with Mom's and Dad's girlfriends, I didn't want to lose either of them over their choices in companions. Mending my relationship with my mom was not going well. Since she'd been back we were distant, and I needed to figure out a way to reconnect before it was too late.

Outside the restoration shop, gravel popped beneath the truck tires. Craning my neck, I fixated on the buckeye. Its spindly leaves and knotted branches intertwined, creating a tent of opaque gloom over Dad's shop and the lawn below. "No light, no cars. It doesn't look like anyone is there."

Dad opened his door and grabbed Geneva's client file. "You two stay here. I'll check."

"She's my mother."

The interior car light shone on Dad's grumped face.

"Betts slapped me, not you, and I'm the one who found Geneva's file. I should be there to confront them."

I squeezed out the driver's side. Dad didn't try to stop me, and I guessed that secretly, he didn't want to do this alone.

Still seated in the front of the truck, Travis seemed unsure whether or not this was a family-only meeting.

"Come on in the shop," Dad told Travis. "You can wait downstairs while Rachael and I check the apartment."

He punched the code, and high-pitched beeps disarmed the alarm system. I flicked a set of lights, and Travis settled on a stool near the Tiffany chandelier.

"We shouldn't be long," Dad said.

"When you rekeyed the locks last Christmas, did you rekey this one?"

His face frumped, and he blew out steam. "Only the external locks. No one ever stays here, so I didn't think I needed to." He held his voice low. "Travis, would you do us a favor? If you hear Maeve and Betts arriving, call up to us."

He and I climbed a set of stairs. "Do you think they're here?"

Holding his key chain, Dad knocked. "No, we'd hear them, and a light would be on. "Maeve? Are you in there?" he called as he unlocked the door and switched a light.

A patchwork quilt had been pulled taut under the pillows. The apartment air was muggy, but smelled lemony. Someone had recently cleaned.

There weren't any suitcases or personal items. Two notes rested on top of the pillows, one to me and one to Dad. We sat on the bed, each with an unopened note.

"They've left," he said.

"I figured that one out."

Dad hugged me. When he released, he wiped a strand of hair from my face and lifted up his note. "Shall we?"

I nodded, and we both opened our Dear Johns. Mine took seconds to read. I placed it in my lap. "What did yours say?" I asked.

"It was vague. Said she's glad to see we're doing well, thanked me for letting her stay, and said she'd be in touch. What about yours?"

"It's an impersonal apology. Said she's sorry Betts and I didn't have a more agreeable meeting."

Dad scowled. "That's it?"

"She said she came to town with righteous intention, and that she hopes someday I'll understand."

"What?" Dad asked.

I handed him the note, and he read over it, twice. "Rachael, something we don't understand is going on inside your mother's head."

The two of us walked around the apartment. It didn't appear as though they'd left any belongings behind. I opened the drawers and checked the medicine cabinet and the shower stall. The space was cleaner than when they'd arrived. Dad stood in front of the window near the buckeye tree and took out the bent screen. Somewhere in the distance rockets began to pop and whistle.

I sat at the small secretary desk in the corner and began opening the stacked drawers. The piece used to be in our house, and I remembered the hidden drawer across the bottom. I tapped at the corner and it opened. It was empty except for a yellowed piece of parchment paper with a black-and-white astrological drawing. I tapped Dad on the shoulder and handed it to him.

He moved toward the light. "It's a constellation." He dragged his finger across the page. "The center is Ophiuchus. Below are Sagittarius, Scorpio, and Libra."

"Ophiuchus? The thirteenth sign of the zodiac? Mrs. Curtis mentioned it."

"Who is Mrs. Curtis?"

"Trudy's neighbor. Do you think Betts left it behind?"

"Not sure."

"That's weird."

Dad grimaced. "Come on, let's get out of here."

Back in the shop, Travis was bent over a worktable rubbing his fingers against a pile of metal beads that had been melted by a solder gun. "Find anything?" he asked.

I shook my head. "Just Ophiuchus."

"Who?"

Dad opened a desk drawer and lifted out a pair of reading glasses. I turned on the banker's glass lamp, and he nodded thanks. "The vellum's not singed. I can make some inquiries at the planetarium. Ophiuchus. Serpent-bearer," Dad whispered. "The sixty-ninth plate in the lost book of Nostradamus."

Inside my brain resistors, transistors, capacitors, inductors, and diodes surged. "Dad, you and I both know that book isn't lost."

In dead silence I listened to him swallow.

"The age of spiritualism has transcended into Canton," Travis said.

Dad's head popped up. He walked across the shop and tugged a cloth off an easel. Geneva's painting, *Cassandra of Troy*, was gone.

NOTE TO SELF

Holy shit, my mom and Betts ripped us off. I hope there's another explanation, but I can't think of one.

11

Parallels

I'd been awake for hours when sunlight began to streak under my bedroom shade, sending crisp snaps of the morning air into my head. It was going to be the kind of day that I should spend at a lake working on my tan. But that wasn't going to happen. The bottoms of my bare feet rested on the wall, and I searched the plaster ceiling for answers. My head buzzed with implausible scenarios. Mom and Betts, art thieves? Had they planned to rip Dad off all along? Betts said she liked to live an unmaterialistic life and that she wasn't a collector. What a crock of swamp shit. Betts was capable of theft. *But Mom?* I couldn't wrap my head around that. I wanted to believe that she was a victim.

Assuring me it wasn't my company, Travis decided on an early start home. Wanting to see him before he left, I got out of bed and slipped on a pair of knee-torn Levi's jeans. Something inside a pocket dug into my hip. It was the crystal Mrs. Curtis had given me, and it sparked an idea. I knew where to go to get answers. Travis and I needed to visit the psychic expo to prove Mom's innocence.

A nutty aroma wafted its way upstairs. Dad was the only coffee drinker in the house. As my feet touched the first-floor landing, I immediately noticed the sofa was empty, and I fumed. Had last night's drama opened Dad's bedroom door for Trudy? I knew they had to be doing it, but I preferred the curtain of innocence they'd kept in front of me. Inside the kitchen, I sighed. Dad was wrapped behind a newspaper. He tipped the last drips from his mug into his mouth. I looked at the empty twelve-cup coffee maker pot. Sliding in the seat next to him, I asked, "Where's Trudy?"

Resting the paper on the table, he moved to the counter and began measuring grounds into a new filter. "She's subbing for the seven thirty class."

His tone was distant, and I had enough experience to know his mood teeter-tottered between polite and pissed. It was the waiting that bothered him. It bothered me, too.

"Did you leave Edmond a message?"

He nodded.

Edmond was the only person who may have a reasonable explanation for the missing *Cassandra* painting. Unfortunately, he was camping in his tin can on wheels and wouldn't be back until tonight.

"Geneva asked me if I'd catalogue her library books. I'm supposed to go over Monday morning."

Dad's hand slammed the counter. "Why didn't I know about this?"

Jeez, he was edgy. "She asked me when Edmond and I picked up the *Cassandra*. Her library's been painted. She has a bunch of first editions. Dynasty Asian and early European-bound manuscripts in boxes on the floor. I thought it would be kind of fun. She said she'd pay me double what you do."

Dad scoffed. "Did she?"

"Should I cancel?"

Rubbing newly formed creases in his forehead, he said, "I don't want you working for Geneva."

"Why?" *It's not your fault the painting was stolen.*

He poured water into the Mr. Coffee, and the machine sputtered. "We won't know if the painting is actually missing until I speak to Edmond."

"Maybe Edmond delivered it early. Why not call Geneva and ask?"

Dad winced. "I don't want to concern her until I'm sure of what we're dealing with. If Edmond doesn't know where it is, then I'll file a police report and call the insurance company Monday morning."

Words came out of Dad's mouth, but his mind seemed adrift. I got the feeling there was something else going on, but didn't know what.

I plucked Dad's truck keys from the hook next to the kitchen pocket door. "I'm going over to Trudy's apartment to hang with Travis before he leaves. Probably get some breakfast."

Moving toward the picture window behind the kitchen table, he stared out at the morning.

"I may run an errand," I said. "See if I can catch a con."

"Have a good time, and tell Travis it was a pleasure meeting him. He's welcome back anytime."

WE'D DRIVEN SEPARATELY. In the expo parking lot I slid into Travis's Volvo passenger seat, and I handed him a fast food bag. He crinkled his nose toward my breakfast sandwich. "You don't have egg on your Egg McMuffin?"

"I order it without."

"But it's an Egg McMuffin. It should have egg," Travis said.

He had this way of contorting his mouth when I surprised him. The seemingly small facial maneuver oozed sex appeal, making me forget he was gay. *My hormones are out of control.*

"Some night," he said.

"Life is full of surprises. I'd never have pegged my mom a lesbian thief who'd rip off my dad's restoration artwork."

"Hey now," he said.

"You know what I mean. She lived a quiet heterosexual life for twenty years and then goes all experimental."

"She may have been experimental all her life and just kept it hidden." Travis was right. I didn't know.

"Do you really think your mom and Betts stole the *Cassandra* painting?"

"I don't want to believe they did, but we're dealing with a woman who created a business model to take people's money by reading 'auras.'"

We walked through the convention center parking lot toward the entrance. Travis told me, "This is America, birthplace of the pet rock, Mexican jumping bean, and all things gimmicky. If someone is willing to pay for her service, then who can blame her? Betts is an entrepreneur."

I threw my paper bag in the garbage can and drained my Diet Coke. Twirling the talisman I wore around my neck between my fingers, I said, "Betts isn't an entrepreneur. She's a crook, and I don't like her. Let's see what's going on at their booth."

Travis stopped walking. "That's it, that's your plan?"

"Do you have a better idea?"

"No."

The two of us followed a worker who pushed a metal cart on wheels toward the front door of the building. He held the door, and we both slipped inside.

"Rachael, we need to strategize this through. I mean you don't just think that your mom and Betts will be in the booth and that they'll confess to taking the *Cassandra*."

I grimaced.

"You presume you can talk them into returning the painting?"

He had exposed my nonplanned plan. I didn't have a speech prepared. If they were here, I'd keep a stick's length away from Betts and ask Mom for answers.

We passed a stand selling runes and another one specializing in feng shui home consultations. I could see the neighboring booth I'd crawled into last week. The assorted whimsical angels hung from a twinkling ceiling. My Egg McMuffin without the egg lodged inside my chest. "I just want to see if they're here...doing anything unusual."

"Unusual? Rachael, have you forgotten we're at a psychic expo?"

The convention didn't open until nine. Only a handful of people, mostly employees, walked around vacuuming the aisles and collecting garbage.

We gawked at the backside of someone dressed in black, stacking cans into a pyramid on a table. A banner read *Energy Boost, Exclusive Offer.* "Sky, what are you doing here?" Travis asked.

I knew exactly what she was doing here.

"Open that case for me, will you?" she asked.

"Did you get permission?" I asked.

"I told Betts and your mom all about Energy Boost. Betts said I could set up on the last day."

"Really?" my voice squeaked.

"Do you know what kind of foot traffic this place gets? Thousands. I had this banner made," she said, flicking it.

"Don't you think the expo police are going to notice that you commandeered the aura reading booth?" Travis asked.

Sky cracked her gum and twirled the orange piece of hair near her face. "I thought Rachael's mom and Betts would be here. Where are they?"

Travis kicked a black plastic garbage can in the back of the booth. "They sure cleared out fast."

When the can tipped over onto the carpet mat, tea spilled out of a cup, and an empty plastic bag stuck to it. I recognized the stamped logo. *Herbal-U,* and beneath it was printed *African Ginger Powder.* Maybe this visit wouldn't be a total bust.

CONVENTION PATRONS WHO HADN'T OVERDONE the Fourth drizzled into the parking lot. Travis stood next to his car, and I hugged him, letting my arms linger on his broad back. I fantasized he'd drop his gaydom, which was probably as likely as Simon Le Bon calling me onstage at a Duran Duran concert. Travis turned the Volvo engine over and wound down his window. With Dad's truck keys in my hand, I waved as he pulled out. "Call me when you get home."

My heart pumped and my palms were clammy. Zorro, i.e., Jackson Kimball, knew more than he'd let on about Betts. I was sure of it.

Entry was free until noon. I was surprised how many people wanted to know how to avoid misfortunes in their lives. Personally, I lived by a trial and error instinct, and my instinct told me that Jackson Kimball's cute ass had a tale to tell.

WATCHING SOMEONE BENT OVER a case of sealed herbal bags reveals a lot. For instance, the green-and-blue-plaid-tartan fabric that poked out of his pants told me that Jackson wore boxers, not briefs. He wasn't wearing his Zorro getup, but a more relaxed jeans and tee. His butt was square-ish firm, not melonesque, and not old man flat. There was a faded circle the size of a biscuit cutter on his back pocket. On a scale of ten, I'd score the rear view of his 506 Levi's a nine.

I walked behind him and cleared my throat.

He swiveled his head, and a playful smile twisted the corners of his mouth. "Rachael O'Brien."

"I was just passing by and thought I'd say hi."

His lingering eyes made me fidget, and I kicked at imaginary ants with the toe of my shoe.

"Have you been staying out of trouble?"

"I haven't been in any girl fights since I last saw you."

He moved close, and I stepped back. "May I?" Tilting my head in his hands, he examined the area where Betts had slapped me. I drank in his sweet cologne and felt warm under his touch. "I don't see bruising. Did you use the lavender oil?"

"I did. Thanks for the sample."

"So what can I do for you? Or is this a social call?"

Leaning my fists and backside against a table stacked with boxes, I said, "African ginger."

He narrowed his eyes. "Powder or root?"

"Powder. I want to buy some."

"What symptoms are you havin'?"

"It's not me, it's my dad's girlfriend. She's been staying with us and"— I looked left then right and whispered—"her intestinal tract is not right." I waved my hand in front of my face. "She's a health nut. Drinks sardine and seaweed smoothies. Won't take anything over the counter. I remember you mentioning the African ginger. I thought it would sort her out."

Jackson stepped in close. His hand swept a lock of hair that had escaped my ponytail. "I can help you with that, but not right now. I sold out before dinner last night. I have another shipment being overnighted."

I looked up into his eyes. "How much will that cost?"

"I'll give you a good price. Three ounces, eighty-five grams, for—" he said, and kissed me.

Our sudden connection was like a hot brain freeze that caught me off guard in a good way. His hand slid down my neck. My hands didn't know where to go and gripped the table edge. I probably should've pushed him back. Told him how inappropriate kissing a complete stranger was. But I forget all that, as well as my middle name, my age, and why I was here.

"Excuse me," some inconsiderate stranger interrupted. "Do you have water hyssop?"

Jackson stepped back, and I gawked at him. His face. His coffee eyes. He caught my glance, and I dropped my stare to his t-shirt logo. It was a faded picture of a store on the end of a dock, an ice machine resting beside the front door. Below the scene, it said, *Marina Supply*. I squinted at the next line where a screen-print letter was missing. *New -ern, NC.*

"*Bacopa monnieri*," Jackson said. "Also called Brahmi and thyme-leafed gratiola."

My mind whirled in a cranium explosion. Holy doo-doo, I'd just swapped spit with freakin' Bubba Jackson whose specialty, besides being a complete hottie, was running a drug ring. And as a hobby, he moved forged paintings for his fucked-up friend, Billy Ray.

Hopping to my feet, I tapped my Swatch and motioned to leave. Jackson stretched his arm, and his fingers handcuffed my wrist. My eyes trailed up his shapely biceps. A small tattoo of a leaf with jagged edges crept out of his sleeve. "Don't leave."

"I have an errand to run. I'll be back."

The customer in the booth asked Jackson if he knew for certain that the water hyssop was Sri Lankan. Jackson released my wrist, and I slipped

out. I willed myself not to run until I turned a corner. Then I sprint-
ed out the nearest exit and didn't stop until I sat inside Dad's truck. I
flinched my eyes up and scanned the rearview mirror wondering if he
had followed me.

I PANTED LIKE A DOG as I hustled to get inside my house. Voices
echoed from the kitchen. Edmond and Trudy stood in front of the island as Dad paced with a phone cord trailing behind him. "This is John
O'Brien," he said into the phone. "I own How's Your Art, O'Brien's Fine
Restoration. I want to report a theft."

"You're back early," I told Edmond.

He held a mug of coffee and took a sip. "Left this morning. Wanted
to beat holiday traffic."

"You got Dad's message?"

He nodded.

"So what's going on?" I asked, already knowing the answer.

"*Cassandra* is gone," Trudy said.

Edmond cleared his throat. "After you left with Travis, I cleaned the
canvas and touched up some frame nicks with gold leaf. I put her on the
easel to dry before I left for the weekend."

"John's reporting the theft to the police," Trudy whispered.

"Did you set the alarm?" I asked Edmond.

"I did after I spoke to your mom and Betts."

"What?" I asked.

"They drove up as I wheeled my bike out front. I started talking with
them, and they followed me inside the shop."

"What did you talk about?" I asked.

"The heat, my camping trip." He took another sip, staring at me.
"Your mom asked how you and your dad have been getting along."

I didn't think Mom cared.

I wanted to know precisely what was said, but not with Trudy around.
"Do you think they stole the *Cassandra*?"

Edmond wore a worried look. "I hate to think so, but…"

"But what?" I asked.

"It didn't seem significant at the time." His mouth tightened. "Betts went up to the apartment from inside the shop. When she returned, we all went outside, and I locked up and set the alarm."

"How could they steal the painting? If they went into the shop, the alarm would've triggered."

"I didn't check the inside door to the apartment. Betts could've left it open. The alarm is rigged to perimeter doors and windows. If someone was already inside, it wouldn't go off."

Dad gave the address of the shop to the officer on the phone line and hung up. "A detective is meeting me at the shop. Edmond, he'd like to get a statement from you."

I handed the truck keys to Dad. He walked out the front door with Edmond and Trudy. "Rachael, lock the door behind me."

I didn't hesitate to turn the dead bolt. As soon as I heard the truck engine start, I ran upstairs to find a phone number and dialed. I called Katie Lee first, but no one answered. After leaving a message, I dialed another number. The phone rang five times until someone picked up. "Is Patsy there?"

There was a pause. "Rachael?"

"Mitch?"

"Hey, darlin', how's your summer goin'? Been stayin' out of trouble?"

"Kind of," I said, and he laughed. "What about you? Anything going on?"

"Nothing like when you come to town."

I'd forgotten Mitch's charm.

"So when are you coming to The Bern?"

"Once I get back to campus, I'm sure Katie Lee and I'll plan a roadie."

"I'll look forward to that. Patsy's not around. Not sure where she is."

I sighed. "You knew Bubba Jackson, right."

"Yeah."

"Has he turned up in town at all?"

"He bolted. No one's seen him since the epic night of the McGees' party."

"Could he pass as Zorro? Did he ever wear a black silk shirt with a tied sash?"

"Rachael, have you been smokin'?"

"Mitch, I think he's in Canton. What's his last name?"

"We just call him Jackson."

Not exactly helpful.

"What does he look like?"

"Damn, girl. I don't know. He's a guy."

"Brown hair and eyes? Tanned olive skin, fit."

"I guess."

"Does he have a tattoo of a cannabis leaf on his left arm?"

"I don't know. Hold on." Mitch shouted to one of his brothers, "Does Jackson have a hooch leaf tattoo?"

I heard the answer the same time Mitch did. "Yeah, on his left arm. He has a badass one on his lower back of a guy with a beard holding a serpent. Says it's the thirteenth zodiac sign."

"Ophiuchus."

A SUN-BAKED BREEZE billowed from beneath my bedroom curtain, then clunked the weights sewn in the hem against the wall. On top of my dresser a fan droned as it moved air against my skin. Did I wear a sign on my back that said, *Loser, please take advantage*? How could I be so stupid? Jackson must've known who I was all along. Did he come to Canton for revenge? Luring me so I'd trust him? Then pack me in a crate and dump me off some cliff? Shit, shit, shit. I knew who I should call, but hesitated. I told myself I'd wait to get a full report from Dad before I contacted FBI Agent Storm Cauldwell.

It was past lunchtime, and I'd organized my sock drawer and ponytail holders, and smoked half a pack of cigarettes. I'd started arranging my shoes by color and heel height when the phone rang. It was Dad checking on me. He said they were wrapping things up at the shop and that he would be home within the hour.

"Do the police think Betts stole the painting?"

"I've filed a report, and Edmond gave them a detailed description of the events before we discovered the missing painting. They said they would look into Betts's possible connection, but would need probable cause before they could get a search warrant. Rachael, there's a chance your mother is involved."

Hanging up, I wondered if this day could get any worse. My hand still rested on the phone when it rang again. I answered it greedily, thinking Dad forget to tell me something important.

"Rachael?" A southern voice asked, and I immediately felt guilty.

"Clay?"

"Did I catch you at a bad time? I mean are you busy?"

"No," I said, my voice pitching up an octave.

After an awkward pause I blurted, "Sorry about that interruption the last night on campus, but I had no idea that Agent Cauldwell was going to show up. I would've stayed except he's FBI. I mean he needed a statement, and I didn't think it would be wise to piss off a fed."

"You don't need to apologize. I'm the one that... What I wanted to say was, I've missed you. I'm sorry I didn't call sooner."

MIDAFTERNON DAD AND TRUDY returned to the house, and the three of us sat at the picnic bench out back. With all the drama, Dad loosened his rein on alcohol consumption. He and I drank Iron City, and Trudy sipped a protein-boost-powder-lemonade concoction through a straw while she thumbed the crime blotter of the Sunday paper.

I wasn't sure if the missing *Cassandra* painting—possibly stolen in a vendetta by my mother—outweighed having kissed Jackson Kimball, a.k.a. Bubba Jackson. My memory hovered in fuzzy denial. Did he really kiss me or did I imagine it? Could he be the Bubba Jackson wanted by the FBI for involvement in the New Bern art forgery ring and marijuana operation? No one who is that good a kisser can be Bubba Jackson, the art forger henchman and cannabis smuggler extraordinaire. It was unlikely, *wasn't it*? *Just a coincidence?* Hordes of people probably have marijuana leaf tattoos. The connection wasn't 100 percent, and I talked myself out of calling the FBI contact and bothering him with my imaginative sleuthing. And it wasn't the sort of thing I could tell Dad. *I was messed up. I liked Jackson Kimball.*

"Are we missing something here?" I asked. "I mean is there some-one else who could've stolen the *Cassandra*? Was anything else in the shop missing or displaced?"

Trudy folded the paper and put it on the table. She scrolled an article with her finger. "More home robberies in Stark County. North of here. It says electronics, jewelry, and fine artwork were taken from Maybelle and Samuel Jones, in Norton, and Schmidt and Betty—"

"Bismet?" Dad asked.

Trudy looked up from the paper, "Yeah, in Hartville."

"Do you know them?" I asked.

"May I?" Dad asked, sliding the newspaper toward him. He mouthed over the words in the article before standing up. As he moved toward the house, he said, "They're former clients of mine. I've done painting res-torations for them both."

"Do you think it's related? I mean maybe Mom and Betts didn't swipe the *Cassandra*. Maybe we were robbed."

"I'm calling the detective. This could be significant."

DAD, TRUDY, AND I stayed up late. Our house was like a hotel lobby. A detective and some policemen stopped by. They hadn't found Betts or Mom yet. They wanted to know what work Dad had restored for the two couples whose homes had been robbed. Dad ended up going over to the shop to Xerox their files.

Trudy and I were sitting outside not saying much when gum cracking startled me. "Jesus, Sky, what are you doing here?" I asked.

"Just in the neighborhood."

The wine I'd been drinking had relaxed my word filter. "What hap-pened? You look like you were abducted into another realm?"

"I sold out at the expo."

"Fantastic! How many?" Trudy asked.

She plopped onto the picnic bench. "Thirty cases."

"Whoa, how'd you do that?"

"I set up at eleven and sold everything I had by one. A cute guy from another booth wiped me out."

"I'm impressed." *And I was.*

CRICKETS STRUMMED A STEADY beat when Sky left our house. I was edgy. There was no way I could sleep until I had a detailed description of Bubba Jackson. I dialed Katie Lee's number, and this time she answered.

"Hey, Rach. What's going on?"

"I have a question. Does Bubba Jackson have a tattoo on his bicep of happy grass, and have you ever seen him dressed like Zorro?"

"Lord, Rachael, where do you come up with this stuff?"

I twisted the phone cord. "I'm serious. Patsy said he was a redneck. What's so redneck about him?"

"She said that?"

"Yeah."

"She must've been mad at him. He doesn't sport a mullet or live in a trailer and eat pig's feet or any of that. Jackson's smart, really smart. Definitely one of the boys, big partier, always has the best weed."

"Does he own a herbal company?"

"Apparently a cannabis one, judging by what they found in his kitchen cabinets and freezer."

"What's his last name?"

"Kimball, but everyone calls him Bubba Jackson."

Conversations with Katie Lee tended to drain my head, leaving it in a vegetablelike state. This one was no different. My life had altered the moment I met her in Grogan Dorm hallway last fall, and I wasn't sure if I could categorize the "change," under positive. My alarm bells rang and my conscience shouted, make the phone call.

NOTE TO SELF

Why can't the whole New Bern art scam thing just go away? If I call FBI Agent Cauldwell, he's going to think I like him. Which I do, but he's not right for me. He's bossy, licensed to kill, and is way older than me.

12

Stew Me in a Saucepan

Unwilling to give way to sunlight, late morning hovered in a state of gloom. The day and my mood were indecisive, caught somewhere between wanting and not wanting the conse-quences that came with a package of clarity. Guilt surrounded me from all sides: my secret addiction to cigarettes, my wayward mother, my inability to accept her psychic-lesbian lifestyle, and Jackson Kimball, the swindling, drug-dealing, amazing kisser who was wanted by the FBI. Like my nicotine-packed cigarettes, I had a weakness for Jackson. I knew it was wrong, but he'd seemed legit at the expo. He just happened to have a side business selling forged painting and illegal herbs. I was attracted to him and struggled to make the phone call that would put him behind bars.

Dad drove the speed limit and stopped for a full four seconds at every intersection. He took his time driving to Geneva's, and when he pulled in at a gas station to fill the van, I asked, "Are you sure you want me there when you tell her the painting has been stolen? I mean I don't really know her. What if she flips out?"

The gallon numerals incrementally raced inside the glass face of the Arco pump. Through an open window, he said, "This is family business. You're old enough to be involved in the good and the bad. If you want to own your own gallery someday, you're going to have to learn the responsibility of taking ownership."

He finished pumping gas and continued the drive to Geneva's house. The work van doors snapped closed, announcing our arrival. As we walked across a cobbled path to the door, I looked toward the orchid house, but didn't see Geneva. She was expecting me to log her books and manuscripts. She'd be surprised to see Dad. They rarely spoke, and I didn't know why. Once he dropped the bomb about the *Cassandra* painting having been heisted from our shop, I figured she'd stop talking to both of us.

Dad signaled for me to ring the bell. I pushed the button and waited.

She opened her door bearing a gold letter opener in one hand and a Phillips screwdriver in the other. "Hello, Rachael." Stepping back, she looked at Dad. "This is an unexpected visit."

"Geneva," he said. "May we come in?"

"Is everything okay?" I asked, eyeing the sharp objects.

She swiveled the tools around in a kung fu maneuver. "I dropped an earring behind the sideboard and was trying to retrieve it."

We followed Geneva into her kitchen. Cut flowers and fern foliage sprawled across the counter near her sink. "Tea?" she asked.

Dad dug his hands in his khaki pants. "This won't take long."

Geneva looked from Dad to me. "Is something going on?"

"Can we sit?" Dad asked.

She led the way to the sun porch and claimed the high-back wicker chair with the worn cushion. Opening a wooden box, she pulled out a cigarette.

Dad's long legs spilled beyond the seat cushion of the wrought iron glider sofa, and I settled next to him. Leaning forward, he rested his elbows on his knees and focused on his shoelaces.

Geneva flicked a lighter. "You have a look of combustion. You may as well tell me before you explode."

"There's been a theft at the shop. The Evelyn Pickering De Morgan. Your *Cassandra* painting has been stolen."

Smoke from her lit cigarette clouded the still air. "Was anyone hurt?"

"No," Dad said.

"Have you contacted the insurance company?"

"Yes, they will be in touch."

Dark circle patches hovered underneath Dad's eyes.

"Have you filed a report with the police?" she asked.

Dad nodded.

"Do you have any leads?"

My father pushed both hands through his hair. "Yes."

"Who?"

"Maeve and her psychic friend, Betts."

Geneva slammed her cigarette box lid shut and stood up. "John James O'Brien, I told you that woman was trouble, and you went and married her anyway." She stalked across the room, her cigarette affixed between her fingers. Stopping to inhale, she trapped the smoke deep into her lungs.

"Geneva," Dad said in a dangerous tone.

Turning to face him, she pointed the lit tobacco at him. "Don't you 'Geneva' me. Maeve meddled between us, interfered with the business. You always sided with her. This time she's run away to play gypsy, but in Maeve fashion returns to steal from us."

Who did she think she was, telling my father off?

"The police aren't certain."

Geneva pointed her cigarette at me. "She's kept me from Rachael all these years. I always knew she was trouble."

"Mother, that's enough."

TREE CANOPIES ON THE narrow two-lane highway threatened to swallow each corner I turned. Static ran through my head. I'd lost it. Dad, Geneva, Mom, Edmond. They'd all lied. Not a small white lie, but a big, fat, juicy whopper. And thanks to the missing *Cassandra*, Geneva had let that bit of information out from under the cork. *The irony. Cassandra, the prophetic keeper—and this doozy of a secret.*

Dad called it "holding information for personal reasons." Teary-eyed, my paternal grandmother had hugged me. "I wanted to tell you a thousand times."

I didn't hug her back. How could this acquaintance be my grandmother? She lived in my hometown, mere miles from my house, but I'd never spent one holiday or birthday with her. Missed time wasn't something that could be relived. Mom and Dad had kept her from me, and I didn't know if I could ever forgive them.

The weight of the truth threatened to crush a sense of myself I thought I'd known. Without warning, I'd grabbed the van keys. Instinct propelled my legs, and before either of them knew what I was doing, I ran out of the house. Jumping into the van, I drove aimlessly and ended up on one of my favorite roads. It snaked underneath tree branches that dipped and swayed above like a tunnel of wings. Remote and curvy, I'd practiced driving on this stretch when I had a learner's permit. Before a wooden bridge that crossed the Nimishillen Creek, I pulled the car over. Winding my window down, I stuck my head out and dangled my limp arms. With closed eyes, I fell into a vortex of emptiness and sucked air. When I opened them, my chest constricted and my tear ducts flooded. At nineteen years of age, my life was a magnet for deceit.

I couldn't remember the last time I'd had a decent cry. It didn't flush out all my anger or change the lies I'd been told, but it somehow lightened a burden and made me thirsty. I drove to the 7-Eleven and bought a Coke Slurpee. Dad being stuck at his mom's house gave me a vengeful pleasure, and I wondered what the two were talking about. I hoped that he worried that I'd run away. I wanted him to feel the emotional drain his withholding of information had sucked from me.

HITCHED TO A DOCK, the paddleboats sat idle. Except for the geese on the grassy mound in the middle, the pond at Lakeside Shores apartment complex was deserted. I'd been sitting in the parking lot with the van windows open for over an hour, and as if I'd had an out-of-body experience, I wasn't sure why I'd driven here. A combination of the information I'd recently acquired about my grandmother and the giant Slurpee I'd guzzled sent me into a brain spiral of ifs, buts, and whys. I'd hit bottom when a thump on the passenger door startled me.

"Hey, Rach," Sky said. "What are you doing here?"

I humphed a sigh. "I've been delivered a mother lode of emotional baggage."

She opened the unlocked passenger door and settled into the seat beside me.

"What happened?"

"I've just met my grandmother who I thought was dead."

"Whoa, was she abducted and returned?"

Incongruously I gaped at Sky, then started to laugh. I should've been crying, but I didn't have any tears left. Besides, laughter felt better.

"I don't get it. What's so funny?" she asked.

"Dad and his mom had some kind of epic fight when I was young. My mom caused friction between them, and they stopped speaking, until today."

"Are you serious?"

I nodded. "I didn't think I had a living grandparent. Turns out I do, and I've known her as an acquaintance all my life."

"That's galactic. What are you doing here?"

"I stormed out with the van when they told me. Ended up here."

Sky put a hand on my shoulder. "Is there anything I can do?"

What could anyone do? "Naw. I'll be okay. I just need time to digest."

She dangled a set of keys. "I was going to check Trudy's apartment. We're expecting a shipment of Energy Boost. Wanna come up?"

I nodded. I needed to pull myself together before I drove home.

BROWN CARDBOARD CASES WERE stacked to the ceiling, creating towers on either side of Trudy's open front door. A low hum vibrated out of the apartment. Someone chanted nonsense words I had heard before: "Ocha kiniba nita ochun—cheke." The hallway went quiet until a ting chime pricked my ears. It sounded like pie plates that banged in the wind to scare crows.

Sky held a finger to her lips.

We crept around the stacked boxes and moved closer to the open door. The air smelled sweet and charred. Arm in arm, we tiptoed under crystals that dangled from a ceiling fixture into Trudy's apartment. Throws were folded, pillows had been fluffed, and furniture rearranged since my last visit. The apartment I stood in could have been a model home. *Except model homes don't feature closed-eyed senior citizen healers who wave a wad of burning weeds while drumming bare feet to a tribal rhythm they create in their heads.*

Normally I would have giggled, but Mrs. Curtis leashed such focus, aligning the steps she took with the garble she spoke. Besides thumbing the eye of Horus around my neck, I was mesmerized.

The chanting quickened, the stomping increased, and Mrs. Curtis waved the weeds in larger circles, covering the outer corners of Trudy's combo kitchen, dining, and living room.

Sky cleared her throat. "Ah. Mrs. Curtis."

She stopped what she was doing and smiled. "I've been expecting company."

Her sandy creek bed eyes were glassy, and the braids that she wore twisted into the beehive on top of her head glinted tints of purple. I'd met her twice before and still didn't know if her "hairdo" was real.

As she plucked a carved cane from the corner, her taffeta wrap dress rustled while her bare feet floated across the room. Silently circling Sky and me, twice, she created a ring of smoke.

"Please, call me Saker."

"As in falcon?" I asked.

Mrs. Curtis, a.k.a. Saker, nodded. "Your memory of ancient symbolism is sharp. A gift of your lineage."

"Falcon?" Sky asked.

"In ancient Egypt, it symbolized spirit, light, and the rising sun."

"Whoa," Sky mused.

I swallowed my emotional turmoil about Dad and Geneva. Saker's soothsaying replaced my self-obsessing with a curiosity.

"Why are you in Trudy's apartment?" Sky asked.

"Bad juju lurked within. I could feel it down the hall. It was making me edgy."

Sky wore a look of utter duh, which Saker interpreted as concern. "Don't worry, I've cleansed it."

"By burning weeds and moving the furniture around?" Sky asked.

Pointing to a fish bowl with a blooming water lily, she said, "I've cleared the flow of energy, added more water and earth for balance. Will you girls tell Trudy that she's got boxes exploding into the hallway?"

"Rachael and I were just going to take them to my car."

Mrs. Curtis raised and lowered her head, squinting through thick wire-rimmed glasses. "I haven't seen Trudy all summer. I have a bad feeling."

Me too. One that has lasted ALL SUMMER.

Sky slid a hand on Saker's back, guiding her to the doorway. "She's fine. She's just been busy with work."

"Do you have a key to Trudy's apartment?" I asked.

"Of course. And she has one to mine. For emergencies."

Sky and I walked Saker down the hallway. Cradling her apartment doorknob in one hand, she said, "Thank you, girls."

We watched her enter.

Before she closed the door she gazed into my eyes. "When you stop running you will find deeper meaning and focus in your pursuits. Protective keepsakes such as yours time-travel through gifted hands."

A TACKY SWEAT PASTED my shirt to my skin. Moving the boxes of protein powder from the apartment hallway to Sky's car had stopped the nervous jitter that pulsed inside me and replaced it with fatigue. The encounter with Saker, the healer, had the curious effect of freaking me out. I'd determined it was her eyes that had unsettled me. When I last looked at them they'd turned muddy. Physically she was a senior citizen, but her eyes were like a mood ring that reflected the emotion in the room.

I'd helped Sky load her boxes of protein powder and, on the last trip to her car, asked, "When you were at the expo, did you see a guy who looked like Zorro and spoke with a southern accent? His booth was an aisle away from Betts's called Herbal-U."

"Jackson Kimball?"

My heart skipped some beats. I nodded. "That's him."

"He bought three cases from me. That's a six-month supply. My biggest sale of the day."

"Why'd he buy that much?"

Sky slammed the trunk. "The place was raging, and I thought he was going to resell them once I left, so I didn't ask."

Rays of sunshine broke out of the clouds and beat on my head. I shielded my brow with my hand. "Does the protein powder have other uses?"

Sky grimaced.

"Don't tell me. It cleans stubborn toilet rings?"

"At twelve dollars a can, I don't think anyone would consider flushing it. Jackson told me he'd be going away for a while. Said the Energy Boost will give him the vitamins and minerals that he may be missing."

He knows I made the connection.

Sky nudged me. "Wait till Trudy finds out the neat thief is her neighbor who lives down the hall." She winked. "Her apartment is safe. She can move back in."

Digging in my pocket, I pulled out the van keys.

"Yeah, right."

For as many things that had gone off the rails since Mom had come home to Canton, one thing was back on track. Funny, I expected to feel more glee at the prospect of Trudy moving out of our house.

NOTE TO SELF

I have a grandma and am seriously miffed. All these years I wondered what she'd be like. Now I don't want to know.

A falcon in human form, a.k.a. Saker, a.k.a. Mrs. Curtis, was the dust-bunny-collecting tidy thief. Must remember not to loan my key out. Do you ever know your neighbor?

13

Planned Coincidence

Nineteen years old and I've mastered two defense mechanisms: moping and the silent treatment. Two weeks after the Grandma-is-alive bomb, I'd stealthily employed them, imposing the brunt of my discontent on Dad and Edmond. I still worked at the restoration shop. I'd repaired and upholstered the Louis XIV chairs, which Dad delivered. Work orders slowed, but I took care of the few that came in, answered the phones, organized the invoicing, and made calls to old clients for potential commissions.

Reluctantly I continued to work with Edmond on the Tiffany. Its material brilliance prickled reminders of the lies I'd been told. He didn't push for discussions regarding my mood. He had the patience of a hen on an egg and waited. I kept my sanity by counting down the days until I returned to college for my sophomore year. Not including today, fourteen were left.

My mom and Betts were still missing. The police had gone to their last known address in Sedona, but the home was deserted. The *Cassandra* hadn't reappeared. A representative from the insurance company had come to the shop to interview Dad, Edmond, and me before visiting Geneva. The painting had been valued in the high six figures twenty years ago, and now her insurance carrier haggled with ours over the current value before any payments would be issued.

Edmond plugged in the Tiffany, and we both gasped at the green glass against the intricate golden frame. "I told Geneva we would deliver it today," he said.

I raised my eyebrows. "We?"

"It's delicate; I could use a hand. And since you put as much work into it as I did, I thought you might like to see it once it's installed."

"I don't feel right. Going there."

After unplugging the chandelier, he coiled the electrical cord. "Rachael, I can't pretend to know what you're feeling, but I do know that time moves quickly, especially when you get to be my and Geneva's age. Maybe you should consider giving her a chance to explain."

I bit my cheek. I'd liked Geneva before I knew she was my grandma. I would be lying if I didn't admit that I was curious about her life and the blowout that shattered a mother and son's relationship.

"I'll go."

THE BLOOMS ON THE day lilies and turtleheads had wilted and turned brown against green stalks. Darkness flushed out daylight earlier in the evenings, and lightning bug sightings had become sparse, signaling a close to summer. Edmond and I stood at Geneva's front door. Even though I hadn't done anything wrong, an acidic irritation loomed inside my chest, and I suddenly questioned the sanity of coming here. Excuses to bolt drizzled inside my head. I could faint—too risky; they might make me rest on her sofa. A schedule conflict? I'd have to say hi and bye in the same sentence. The front door opened, and a waft of cold air blew out through the screen.

Geneva looked from Edmond to me. Her cheeks lit up, matching her peony cigarette pants and coordinating silk blouse. She was barefoot and her toenail polish, I noticed, coordinated with her outfit.

A large box rested between Edmond and me. "Geneva," he said. "We've brought you something."

She stared into my eyes. "Indeed you have. Rachael, what a pleasant surprise."

Edmond and I lifted the Tiffany while Geneva held the door open. "Careful, don't trip. I've cleared a path down the hall."

Outside the library, an arrangement of sweet peas and hydrangeas floated in an oversized leaded glass bowl, giving the air a delicate floral scent. Inside, other than the boxes that were stacked in front of the shelves and the missing *Cassandra* painting, the library hadn't changed since my last visit. We put the chandelier box down, and Edmond asked where she wanted it. She pointed to the ceiling above a corner table anchored by two chairs.

"I'll need my toolbox and a ladder before I turn the power off," he said.

"Come with me, Rachael. Let's put the kettle on while Edmond gets started."

She backtracked toward the kitchen, and I trailed behind. She poured water into the teapot. "When do you go back to school?"

Leaning against the Formica counter, I said, "Fourteen days."

After placing cups on saucers, she motioned for me to follow her into a back bedroom. "There's something I wanted to show you." Geneva rattled around in a drawer and pulled out a photo. She handed it to me. It was black and white of a girl my age, with short hair, in a flapper dress. I fixed on her smile. It was one I recognized. *My own.* The same lips, same opening, and same crooked eye tooth. Questioningly, I looked at her. "That's me in New York when I was your age."

"But the tooth," I said, looking at her.

She rubbed her tongue along her front teeth. "These are capped." She settled on the edge of the bed. "I worked at the *New York Morning Journal.*"

"The one owned by the newspaper magnate?"

Geneva nodded.

"The antiques, paintings." I eyed the necklace she wore. "Your jewelry?"

"I traveled to Europe and India for him. While I took care of arrangements for his collections, I made a few acquisitions of my own."

"Why did you and Dad stop talking?"

The kettle whistled.

She struggled to choose words. "It was different back then. We are Catholic. Maeve was Protestant." Her tongue stopped. "It wasn't accepted. Honestly, I never liked her. John changed when he met her. I'm one to voice my opinion. Our words escalated, and eventually we stopped talking." She placed a hand on my leg. "Rachael, I'm sorry. I never meant for it to become such a big thing. Our argument grew larger than the both of us, and neither of us knew how to stop it. Will you forgive me?" Tears welled in Geneva's eyes.

A frog stuck in my throat. I threw my arms around her and squeezed. "You're forgiven."

NOTE TO SELF

Family drama and then some. Would like to think this is the last of it, but until Mom is found, I know better.

14

Cleansed and Feng Shui'd

oughy cinnamon buns rose in the oven. I mixed butter, pecans, and brown sugar in a saucepan and stirred the gloppy topping as it melted. When the rolls came out, I'd baste them and then bake them for another five minutes. Two things in particular had swung my mood from flushed down the toilet to rising euphoric. Finding Saker in Trudy's apartment had solved the tidy mystery. Sky had told Trudy and Dad about the encounter while I was with Edmond delivering the chandelier to Geneva's. Trudy shrugged the incident off, apparently not overly bothered now that she knew it was Mrs. Curtis who cleansed the spirits and feng shui'd her dwelling.

Dad wasn't amused and changed Trudy's locks. Medicine balls, Lycra bodysuits, and funky herbs had been transported from our house back into hers. Instantly I liked Trudy a whole lot more and decided to bake gooey, pound-of-butter rolls for her and Dad. I knew it would push her nutrition conscience over the edge and figured they'd slow her down in step class. It was sneaky of me, but I needed an edge. I'd kept my promise by joining her and Dad three times a week in class. They kicked my butt, and now it was a matter of saving face. I couldn't have these two more fit than me. I made an extra batch to split between Edmond and Grandma Geneva. I'd lost my mom, for now, but had found a grandparent.

My afternoons were spent at Geneva's, cataloging the books in her library—taking photos, noting editions, and looking up estimated values, before organizing them on her shelves by century and continent. She had traveled the world on private planes and boats to acquire art, furniture, sculptures, jewelry, and books for her billionaire employer. When we were alone on the sun porch or in the library, she'd told me that she'd been paid well, invested smartly, and made enough contacts to negotiate personal business dealings that allowed her to acquire antiquities of her own. A conversation with Geneva was like sipping old scotch. The different regions she'd traveled produced unique, textured adventures. With attention to detail and a quick wit, she spoke of where she'd gone and the items she'd searched for. She turned her stories into a game that kept me guessing. My conclusions mostly landed in the outfield, but when I was right her eyes sparked, coating me in satisfaction.

Geneva rested behind her desk, penning a note. Her handwriting was full of loops and the spacing between words immaculately consistent.

"You know the book in the purple velvet case?"

She looked at me curiously. I went to a box and pointed at d'Orus Apollo *Des notes hieroglyphiques*.

"It's magnificent, isn't it?"

"It looks old, like an original work."

She grinned.

"You brought it to our house for Dad when I was a small child. How did it end up back here?"

"Open it."

I peeked inside the middle. "It's a brain fuzzler. A translation of a translation. The French handwriting doesn't have punctuation. It's hard to know where the thoughts start and end. The drawings are Egyptian."

Geneva twirled a ring with gray pearls around her middle finger. "Did you see anything else—notable?"

"The signature. It's Nostradamus."

Geneva clapped.

"Is it authentic?"

"No!"

"Where did you get it?"

"Pour me a drink, dear."

A cart with crystal decanters rested in the corner of the room. "Which one?" I asked.

"Far left. The sherry."

As I pulled off the top, Geneva rested her head back. "It was quite a ruse. My employer at the newspaper was obsessed with Nostradamus and collecting anything related to prophecy. He kept sending me on trips to France, England, and Germany. A rival of his, a steel mogul, was also interested in obtaining pieces of religious significance. There hadn't been any real problems until the two honed in on the original book of Nostradamus."

Handing Geneva her drink, I sat in a chair across from her.

"Things escalated. My hotel room was ransacked, and my driver at that time disappeared." She swirled the dark liquid in the crystal tumbler. Her voice trailed. "Both men wanted the book. My boss, to have something no one else did, and his rival, well, he had entirely different reasons. Something had to be done before anyone got hurt."

"What did you do?"

"I did find the original, but kept it a secret. To end the dangerous pursuit, I had a copy made."

"Why did you need a copy?"

She finished her drink with a deep swallow. "I wanted to end this scavenger hunt, and a copy put them off the scent. Too many people were at risk. I showed my boss and his rival the copy. I told them this was a counterfeit, which of course it is, and kept the original a secret. I worried that they'd find out what I'd done, but they never did."

Geneva stretched out a hand and laid it on my knee. "Rachael, what I'm going to tell you I'm not proud of. It cost me something money could never replace. I'm telling you this so you don't repeat my mistakes. I'm not going to make excuses. I never trusted your mother. I tried to break up my son's marriage."

I squirmed under her warm hand. *Trudy and me. Was I following in Geneva's footsteps? Maybe it's true, the apple doesn't fall far from the tree.* What was I supposed to say to that kind of reveal? Confess that I was scheming the same type of maneuver between Dad and his girlfriend?

"My feelings for Maeve have nothing to do with you. Do you understand that?"

"Why did you mistrust her?"

"It was an instinct. I decided to test her. I dropped this prized book at your house when you were very small. Knowing its potential value, I was sure your mother would try to sell it. She didn't. Your father guessed my plan, and we argued horribly."

I opened the protective velvet cover and turned a page. The vellum wasn't aged, and the smell wasn't musty.

The chair Geneva rested in swallowed her. Her gaze went blank as she searched someplace in her mind. "We've only really begun speaking since *Cassandra* was stolen."

"Do you think my mom stole your painting?"

"It looks that way, and I may have to thank her. I lost Cassandra, but was given something far more valuable. My son and my granddaughter."

Geneva's past blew my mind. "Is that what you thought you were doing? Protecting Dad from Mom?" *Did Geneva know my mother better than Dad and I?* "What if Mom and Betts come to your home and rob you?"

"Rachael dear, don't worry about me. I know how to protect my treasures." A sad smile crept across her face. "Fool me once," she said, "shame on you."

"Twice," I said.

In unison, Geneva and I whispered, "Shame on me."

"What you did to my mom and dad was diabolical."

"I took a foolish risk. If your mother had stolen the Nostradamus, it would've proven my gnawing hunch, but she didn't have a chance. Your father returned the book, and we had a falling out. He cut me off from ever seeing my granddaughter. Your childhood was stolen from me."

I should've felt more relief, knowing the history between Dad and my grandmother, but I had an imagination the size of Texas. I hoped the scenario inside my head was a foolish exaggeration. But I couldn't shake the thought that my mother didn't know the book Geneva had delivered was a fake. What if she'd told Betts about its existence? Betts held an infatuation for spiritualism artifacts. A part of me wondered if she was using my mother as her golden ticket to get at that book.

NOTE TO SELF
The more I know, the deeper a sinking feeling rumbles about Betts's involvement with my mother.

15

Precautionary Measures

The air smelled medicinal, and I wondered why doctors' offices didn't use a citrus or floral cleaner. The biting scent reminded me of the waiting rooms of dentists and optometrists. I actually wished I was visiting one of them for an ailment above the neck, rather than here, at the gynecologist, naked and in a breezy paper gown without a closed front. I had to face it, I was a big girl, nineteen, and I was going to have sex. In case things heated up spur of the moment, I wanted to be prepared. I'd considered buying a box of condoms, but a sexpert New Yorker friend from freshman year once told me that doing it with a condom was like licking a lollipop with the wrapper on.

Sky made the appointment and drove me over. She'd already experienced the womanly exam. Being naked in front of a stranger wearing rubber gloves in an artic cooled room was awkward, but I'd survive. When I spotted the stirrups, I wasn't so sure. No one had ever poked around down there, and I wasn't looking forward to the cold metal tongs Sky had told me about.

Fresh out of medical school, the doctor held a clipboard. Reaching her hand forward, she introduced herself. "Hi, Rachael, I'm Dr. Rivers. What can I do for you today?"

"I want to get the pill."

"Are you sexually active?"

"Not yet," I said, and she checked something off on her clipboard.

"Have you had intercourse?" she asked.

That was personal information. "Unfortunately, no," I mumbled.

She put the clipboard down and looked me in the face. "All right then, I'll write a prescription. You must take it every day for it to be effective. Start it on the first day of your cycle. Is there anything else?"

"Don't I have to do the stirrup thing?"

"Since you aren't yet sexually active," she said, her tongue emphasizing the active, "I don't need to give you an internal exam—unless there's a problem. Like discomfort—burning, itching, or discoloration in your discharge."

Jeez. "Nope."

Dr. Rivers ripped a piece of paper off a pad, and that was that. Outside the waiting room, I waved the prescription at Sky.

"How did it go?" she asked.

"Easier than getting a driver's license."

"Just be careful who you drive with," Sky warned.

While we waited for my prescription to be filled, Sky and I busied ourselves testing neon shades of nail polish. I settled on Don't-Tell-Your-Mama pink and she chose Orange Attitude. After I paid for my purchases, Sky cracked her gum. "Looks like you're good to go."

"Hopefully I'll find a willing participant."

"You and Clay are speaking again. You shouldn't have any trouble."

"I hope you're right. For some reason a magnetic field keeps us apart. There's psycho-ex drama, injuries, or scheduling conflicts. I almost wonder if he and I aren't meant to be."

"You can always move on. What about the FBI guy? You said he was hot."

"When did I say that?"

"The night we spent at Trudy's. You said anyone who can handle a gun should be skilled at handling—"

"I did not say that."

Sky laughed. "What does this Clay have anyway? Why does he have to be the one?"

"I'm drawn to him. The brown flecks in his hazel eyes, and the way his crooked smile creases the corners of his mouth, his southern drawl—the whole package. When I'm around him, everything inside of me pops and sizzles."

"That doesn't sound healthy."

"Trust me. He's the one."

"Obsessions are disruptive. They jostle electrons, unbalance planetary alignments, and turn ordinary situations wonky."

"That sounds like a lecture from Mom and Betts's camp."

"Has anyone found those two?" she asked.

"Not yet. The police think they may show up at another psychic convention, but there are six across the country in September. Crimes of art don't take priority at police stations. The insurance company has more motivation to find the *Cassandra* painting than the police do."

I didn't tell Sky about my hunch. It was wicked, and I weighed the chances of Mom and Betts returning for the *book of Nostradamus*. I hadn't asked Geneva where she kept the original book of prophecies. There were a lot of nuts in the world who would kill for something like that. I hoped she'd loaned it to some museum where it sat behind thick glass, but I doubted it.

NOTE TO SELF
Locked and loaded.

16

Juju

Sky drove us past the man-made toilet bowl lake en route to building nineteen. It was my last day of summer before Dad and I headed to North Carolina. Trudy and Dad were throwing me a luncheon celebration at her place. Now that Trudy lived in her own space, I liked her a lot more. That whole Mrs. Curtis, alias Saker, cleansing thing was wiggie. It would've freaked me out if my stuff had gone through a sage smoke feng shui reorganization.

I hadn't eaten before we left, and my stomach grumbled discontent. I worried that Trudy had blended or whisked something inedible. I asked Sky, "So what's for lunch?"

"Chinese takeout."

Whew.

She cruised into a parking spot next to a covered car. Dad and Trudy stood around smiling, and my heart pumped.

"Holy shit."

"Surprise," Sky grinned.

Launching out of the car, I hugged Dad.

"Now, Rachael, what's all the affection about?"

"John, don't be a tease," Trudy said. "Take off the cover."

"Ta-dah," Dad said, pulling the sheet off the car with a dramatic sweep.

I was speechless. "What is it?" I asked.

"It's a car," Trudy said.

Dad rocked onto his toes. "A vintage 1967 Ford Galaxie."

My voice cracked, "It's pea green."

"Original paint color. Do you like it?"

There are some moments in life when it is appropriate to lie. "I love it. Thanks, Dad," I said and hugged him.

Opening the door, he handed me the keys. I slid into the driver's seat. "Where did you get this?"

He glowed. "A friend of Geneva's."

Great, it had my grandma's stamp of approval.

After everyone had sat inside and sufficiently pawed the lentil bomb, Trudy announced, "Come on, let's go inside and eat."

I lingered in the front seat and asked, "Where are you going to keep it while I'm at college?"

"It's yours. I thought you might like to break it in and drive it yourself."

"Really?"

"Really," he said.

"Okay, who are you and what have you done with my father?"

Dad laughed and handed me an envelope.

"What's this?"

"The commission from the Quesnel painting you refurbished last Christmas. I sold it."

Inside the envelope was a thick wad of green bills. I pulled them out and fanned myself. "Dad, I don't know what to say."

"You don't have to say anything. But I do expect you to spend wisely. And no more spring breaking in New Orleans."

"I'm never going back there."

He motioned toward the building. "Are you coming?"

Zipping the envelope in my jacket pocket, I said, "In a minute."

"See you upstairs."

I couldn't believe it. Dad bought me a car. Not exactly my vehicle of choice, but it was four wheels that I hoped would get me to North Carolina in one piece. I slid my hand across the steering wheel and adjusted the rearview mirror. A white van parked in a spot behind me, and Doneski hopped out of the driver's seat. *Figures.* My day had been going beyond expectations until now. Ducking down, I calculated my chances of running into Trudy's apartment building without being seen. When I heard a knock on the trunk, I realized those odds were zero.

Dickhead Doneski leered into the open window. "What do we have here? A seasick granny mobile?"

Scowling at him, I wound the window up.

He stepped back as I got out of the car.

"Get a life."

"Ouch," he hissed. Disgustingly resourceful, he produced a partially smoked cigarette from behind his ear. "If you were nicer to me, maybe I'd offer you something sparkly at a reduced rate."

"What are you babbling about?"

Reaching into his plaid flannel shirt pocket, he wiggled his fingers beneath a handful of tangled gold necklaces and bracelets.

"What are you? The Avon man for jewelry?"

"Just thought you'd be interested in purchasing a little something for yourself." He dangled a bracelet in front of my face, like a worm specimen. "This one has sapphires. It'd look real nice on your wrist."

Rolling my eyes, my head followed. Avoiding Doneski's face, I twisted away and gazed into the back of the van he drove. Cable wires dangled over stacks of TVs and VCRs. There wasn't any crawl space inside the vehicle. Sweeping my hand over the pile of jewelry and then toward the van, I asked, "You're fencing stolen goods?"

"You make it sound illegal. I'm just recycling used products into cash."

"Sorry, Doneski, I'm a broke student," I said, about to turn on my heel.

"Wanna take a look? I can give you a student discount."

A pesky curiosity moved my feet to the back of the van. I didn't need any electronics. "Doneski," I said, ready to ditch him when I glimpsed the corner of a chunky gilded frame poking out behind a TV. The ornate molding triggered my brain. I knew that frame. Willing my voice not to crack, I looked him in the face. He sucked on the unlit cigarette. "I have a poster that needs a frame. Do you have anything?"

"What poster?" he asked.

This, I knew was a trick question. If I'd said The Cure or U2, he'd scoff at me. I didn't think he was into Jerry Garcia; he was too uptight to be a Deadhead. He made a hobby of hiding in bushes with his BB gun. Got his kicks scaring the crap out of innocent passersby. It clicked. "Guns N' Roses."

"You like Slash?"

"Yeah."

He watched me.

I tapped the face of my Swatch. "Listen, if you don't have anything, no biggie."

"I may have something." There wasn't room to climb in from the back. He moved around the van and slid the side door open.

After a quick look at the license plate, E7C-964, I moved to the open door. "Do you need help in there?"

"Naw, I got it. But there's a painting inside the frame."

I memorized the upside down seventeen-digit VIN number from the left-hand corner of the dash and retreated from the van. Doneski scraped a corner of the frame on the van door, and I winced. He held the backside of a gold leaf frame. I saw the thick wire draped across the back. When he flipped the frame around, my heart did jumping jacks in my chest, and I willed myself to keep a poker face. *Don't panic.*

"You and your dad work on this kind of stuff, don't you?"

"Yeah, we repair things."

"How much do you think this is worth?"

Another tricky question. Did he know what he had? Was he testing me? If I low-balled, would he use it for target practice?

"Paintings are subjective. Depends on how deep a buyer's pockets are. I like the frame. I think Slash would look pretty cool inside there. How much do you want for it?"

"I don't know. My next stop is to meet a guy who said he's interested."

"I've got cash."

Doneski bit on the cigarette filter. "Fifty bucks."

"Fifty? I'm keeping the painting for fifty."

"You can have it. It's some dumb redhead standing on a bunch of rocks."

Sky shouted from Trudy's balcony, "Rachael, lunch is ready."

I reached into the envelope Dad had just given me and handed Doneski a fifty. He passed *Cassandra* to me. "See you around, O'Brien."

I nodded. *Not very likely.*

Mindful of how I handled the frame encasing the six-figure stolen painting, I took the apartment stairs two at a time. Trudy's apartment door was open and I leapt in. As I handed Dad the painting, he swore, "What the hell?"

"Pen, paper," I hiccupped.

Trudy thrust them into my hand. I scratched down the digits. Ohio plates E7C-964. White Ford van, dent on driver side, VIN 1falp62w-4wh128703. "Dad, call the detective at the Canton police department. Tell him I bought the stolen *Cassandra* painting from Markus Doneski for fifty bucks."

I tugged at the curtain that covered the open glass sliders to Trudy's balcony and watched him pull away. He wouldn't get far.

I PICKED AT MY FRIED RICE and moved my sweet and sour pork around my plate. I didn't have an appetite. Mom and Betts hadn't stolen the painting. They'd just left for a new venue, to find a better vortex to practice channeling without saying a proper, in-person good-bye. A feeling nudged at my insides. Something wasn't right. Using the old "I have to pack," I stood to leave, and Dad looked worried. Palming the Galaxie key, I assured him I was okay. Just overwhelmed with getting ready to leave for school the next day and having found the painting in Doneski's van. "I want to get back home, get organized, and relax."

"Do you want me to come with you?"

"I'll be fine."

"Lock the door when you get in the house. I'll be back after I meet with the detective."

Driving my vintage Galaxie through Canton streets, I beeped at anything that moved and rolled through two stop signs. Before closing the front door, I put my keys on the Quaker bench in the entry and noticed a cellophane bag of yellow powder and a small pair of black binoculars with a ripped strap and a chip in the left lens. Bile rose in my throat, and my internal organs froze as I lifted the palm-sized bag. Written in block letters with black ink was a note on the label.

I can't believe you got the Cassandra before me. You should change your name from Raz to Lucky. See you around. JK

The powder was African ginger. The binoculars were mine. Three months ago in New Bern, North Carolina, I'd lost them when I plunged off a second-story balcony into the swimming pool. They'd sunk to the bottom, and there hadn't been time to retrieve them. I was too busy running.

Holy shit! Bubba Jackson was still in business—the business of stolen art—and had left a calling card. I rubbed my thumb over the cellophane bag. He was hot. Great, I was attracted to a southern criminal, a wanted man. I pushed the googlie-goop, lusty feeling that threatened the responsible side of me into a hidden place and slammed the door.

As I ran to the kitchen, my fingers trembled. To steady them, I pulled the pink crystal Mrs. Curtis had given me out of my pocket. Phone tucked under my chin, I rolled it between my fingers and used my right pointer to dial a number I had memorized. FBI Agent Storm Cauldwell answered on the second ring.

"Agent Cauldwell, it's Rachael O'Brien."

"Rachael, good to hear your voice. What's going on?"

"Bubba Jackson kissed me."

I watched the second hand on the kitchen clock tick a few beats.
"Did you kiss him back?"

NOTE TO SELF
Gotta get back to school where I can forget about wanting a wanted man.

An invitation from Paisley Ray

If you enjoyed this or any of my other books, I'd love to hear from you. I answer all my e-mails personally, and if you contact me, I will put you on my mailing list to receive notification of future releases, updates, and contests.

Honest reviews of my books are greatly appreciated. I know you have taken your time to read the novel I have woven and by offering a line or two opinion, you not only help other readers decide if this is something they would enjoy, you help me by giving perspective on the story. Your feedback is invaluable for an indie author.

Visit: HeyPaisleyRay.com
E-mail: Heypaisleyray@gmail.com
Become a fan: Facebook.com/Heypaisleyray
Twitter: @HeyPaisleyRay
Pinterest.com/Heypaisleyray

Acknowledgements

Many thanks to Marcel Bradley, Louella and the Tuesday night writers. Also thanks to the Wikipedia community for their invaluable information on various subjects.

Sneak Preview

THE RACHAEL O'BRIEN CHRONICLES
SHELLED AND SHUCKED

A Novel
by
PAISLEY RAY

"He who hesitates is a damn fool."
~Mae West

AUGUST 1987

1

Ain't He the Bee's Knees

"**S**he's about to be SHELLED and SHUCKED," a southern voice I didn't recognize uttered with amusement. I heard giggles but dismissed the distraction. The background chatter of my roommates at the edge of the Grogan Hall parking lot at North Carolina College was barely audible. The distant conversation blended into the symphony of rhythmic insect chirping that serenaded Clay Sorenson and me as we explored each other's lips.

The late afternoon shadows grew as the sun shifted to the west, but didn't provide relief from the unrelenting Carolina heat. The air hung tacky and stiff, luring the call of male cicadas. Droves of them hummed a mating song that rolled in and out of my ears, like a rising tide pushing ashore. Standing on my tiptoes, my eyes drank in Clay's überfine manliness. My short-sleeved IZOD clung to my spine and chest. The moisture beads that adhered my right hand to his neck and my left to the small of his back emitted primal heat, sweetened by the musky scent he'd showered in. Clay's intoxicating blend rocked my core, blinding my cognitive perceptions and fogging my vision. If this was a precursor to sophomore year, I wasn't sure I ever wanted to become a junior.

Disturbingly, I still held my V-card, but those days were numbered. He was so "The One," and if the interior of my 1967 Ford Galaxie wasn't heaving with college stuff, I would've become a woman on the pea-green plastic backseat, without caring who straggled by.

At nineteen years of age, my inner woman was ready for a wash and wax. It had taken ages for us to hook up, but I wasn't going to dwell. Clay Sorenson, whom I had drooled over for an entire year, liked me now. At the end of last year, we'd parted on a low note. It wasn't my fault that smokin'-hot FBI Agent Storm Cauldwell had interrupted our anatomy session in Clay's dorm room. There had been paperwork that needed to be signed regarding my statement about how Billy Ray, a demented redneck art forger had tried to strangle me. Then there was the stolen Clementine Hunter painting I'd found in Bridget Bodsworth's dorm closet. I'd provided evidence linking them, along with two accomplices, to an art forgery scam.

Despite the restraining order on Billy Ray, I didn't feel warm and fuzzy about being back in the state where I could've been killed. The charges were unresolved, and uneasiness pressed at my nerves. I'd be lying if I didn't admit that Billy Ray scared me, and I wouldn't feel safe until he was put away.

When I'd left Clay's room that last day on campus, the mood between us had soured. We never had the chance to realign before I had to go home to Canton, Ohio, for the summer. He had called me once in July, and the conversation was strained. Last night, before I went to bed, I put on my big girl pants and called him. Before I drove to college, I needed to know where things stood between us. Considering how he now sandwiched my chest against his and the pressure he pushed against me, forcing my Daisy Dukes into the hot metal of the driver door, I think it was safe to assume that he was keen to pick up where we'd left off.

He'd sucked all the moisture off my lips, but I didn't care. I wasn't kidding anyone who passed by. We were more than kissing. He and I dined on full grope with a side order of making out. Clay stopped nibbling on my ear lobe long enough to whisper, "I've missed you. A lot," and I mewed.

Time wasn't something that concerned Francine Battle, and she spoke without rushing her syllables. In a soulful voice that deepened at the end of each word, she said, "Joan Jetteson, I'm goin' to enlighten you, free of charge. That there is a classic textbook case example of uncorked infatuation. Built up most of last year. But that bonne homme never got his planet aligned with Rachael's."

"Bonne homme?" the stranger's voice repeated.

"That's swamp talk," Katie Lee said.

Francine hissed, and though she wasn't in my sight line, I imagined she'd anchored her hands on her hips, and I swear I heard the stomp of a fuzzy slippered foot.

"Stay with me. White boys. They can be slow. Nice to look at, but romantically speakin'—a high percentage are daft."

"Come on, Francine," I heard Katie Lee say. "What do you know about white boys?"

"I'll have you know that I'm not a one-flavor kind of girl. Chocolate may be my first choice, but I'm not opposed to other candy."

Girl Code isn't textbook knowledge. No one sits you down, teaches you the guidelines, and gives you a test. It's innate, genetically wired into females as young girls. I knew damn well that Katie Lee and Francine were hanging out on the perimeter of the parking lot. Since I was occupied, I figured "The Code" would kick in. *When a girlfriend hooks up with a guy she has obsessed over for more than six months, do not UNDER ANY CIRCUMSTANCES interrupt.*

Theoretically, they should've moseyed along and waited for me in the dorm, where I'd debrief them later. That didn't happen. Apparently my roommates are able to recircuit the wiring that would jolt any normal, Girl Code-abiding female. Despite being obviously busy, I was aware that I had yet to catch up after a summer apart. But our meet and greet could wait a little longer.

We reveled on with our long-overdue hello until a sharp voice spoke up in close proximity, making me flinch. "Looks like the wick has been lit. Y'all are swappin' spit like Lowcountry lizards."

A Ralph Lauren perfume cloud choked the air. Enveloping Clay and me, it threatened to sedate us. My sophomore year roommates closed in, and begrudgingly, he and I pulled apart.

"Well, it's about time ya got your northern ass on down here. We've been here for hours," Katie Lee said.

Wiping my lips with the back of my hand, my eyes couldn't help but smile. "Katie Lee Brown," I said as I clasped her wrists and fanned her arms to get a look. "Is that a new sundress?"

Wiggling out of my hold, she twirled. Over the summer she'd lightened her hair with Sun In and lemon juice. As her hair grew longer, dark roots pushed the bleached blonde down her crown.

"Mama bought it for me as a goin' away gift. She sent a little something back for you, too. It's up in our room."

Brushing out a crease below her belt, Katie Lee said, "Clay Sorenson, if you have it in your head that you're gonna hog Rachael this year, you just think again."

A gruff "Ahem" broke in, and then repeated, louder.

Clay leaned back against the car. "Francine."

She stepped forward. "Give a girl some of that cane sugar you're wearin'." Wrapping herself around him, Francine didn't exactly rush to release him.

Sauntering the few steps toward me, she licked her palm and stroked it backward from her temple to just above her ear, smoothing the flyaways that had escaped her modest ponytail. With pursed lips, she lazily dragged her glare from my flip-flops up to my neck, and then halted her gaze.

I fidgeted my fingers against the eye of Horus trinket I wore around my neck and skirted my tongue across my crooked eyetooth. Truth be told, I admired Francine. Her game face was always poised. On the outside she was capable of tucking anyone's tail between their legs and sending them scurrying, but inside she was sweet, light, and fluffy, like cotton candy.

"You been down here five minutes and sprouted a hickey on your neck as wide as the Mississippi."

My cheeks felt warm, and I guessed they flushed crimson. "Francine," I garbled.

A girl I hadn't met pressed and released a pocket of metal on the hood of my car, making a popping noise, like it was air-filled Bubble Wrap. A head taller than Katie Lee or me, and two heads taller than Francine, she had stud earrings around most of her left ear. Her purple bangs were blunt and only covered an inch of forehead. The rest of her hair was black and touched her shoulders. My stare lingered on her hands. The skin around her short nails was reddened and cracked. They looked like they'd been through a cold Ohio winter, and I wondered what she'd done over the summer.

The pea-green Galaxie wasn't my first choice in a vehicle. To be honest, it hadn't been on my wish list at all, but it was transportation. The car had three things going for it: it was a gift and, therefore, free; all its parts were where they should be—no hanging tailpipes or broken door handles; and when I turned the key, it religiously started without complaint. I didn't need to start the year with a dent above my engine.

"Easy on that hood," I said.

Katie Lee tugged the southerner forward. "Rachael, this is Joan."

Standing in close proximity to Clay, I had trouble focusing. My hormones still sparked, and the name didn't register in my head bank.

"From the South Carolina Lowcountry," Katie Lee said.

I looked to Francine for a clue. She didn't bother to shield her combo eye-head-roll maneuver. "Our assigned roommate in the quad."

"We've been here most all day," Katie Lee scolded. "Already have everything sorted. It's completely spacious compared to the room we shared last year."

Francine stared at Clay, but her words were meant for me. "Since you weren't here, we made an executive decision and put you on a bottom bunk. As a safety precaution."

I rubbed the walnut-sized lump that had taken up permanent residence on my collarbone. The freshman year memory of free falling off a top bunk was not one of my favorites. The only positive of that day was meeting Clay in the campus infirmary where he was interning.

Stepping toward me, Joan curled the corners of her lips. The right of her mouth tilted slightly higher than the left, giving her a mischievous sneer. Extending her hand toward mine, she gripped my clammy palm and tightened her sandpaper grip. "You've got some rust under the hood. You need to scrape and patch it, otherwise it'll spread like a fungus. Joan Jetteson," she said, putting a twang on the *te* in Jetteson. "Might as well call me Jet; everyone else does."

She released my hand, and it flopped to my side. Realizing I was surrounded by southern, I tried not to arc my eyebrows too close together. *How come I end up rooming with the quirky ones?*

"Do you fly airplanes?" Clay asked.

Sweeping a gaze over him, she shrugged. "I'm attracted to anything with nuts and bolts."

Sidestepping toward Clay, I coiled my arm around his and slinked my hand into his pant pocket. Tangling his fingers around mine, he squeezed away my insecurity. After giving Jet a once-over glance, I decided the chances of having another year of demented encounters had to be zilch. Besides, freshman year had opened my eyes *and* my can of whoop ass. Clay Sorenson and I had chemistry. I planned to christen my sophomore year and sleep with him before the day ended. I wasn't going to let this rust expert interfere.

NOTE TO SELF
Clay is even hotter. I think it's his summer tan.

Joan Jetteson, a.k.a. Jet. Not convinced her nuts and bolts are secure. Proceed with caution.

2

Shooin' Flies

The quad we were assigned was in the same tower building as last year, Grogan. And same as last year, the structure still lacked two essential comforts: carpeting and air-conditioning. This year our two-room living space was on eight, the top floor. I couldn't complain too much since we had a northern bird's-eye view of Campus Drive and, directly below, a crown of waxy green leaves blanketing soaring oak limbs.

The first room you entered from the hallway was where my room-mates had put all our desks. The second space was a catch-all for every-thing else: beds, closets, a sofa, TV, and Francine's lavender butterfly chair that rested on a collapsible metal frame. Katie Lee had brought a giant industrial fan, the type a contractor would use to dry a flooded basement. With the girls' and Clay's help, it only took two trips to move my stuff in.

Before Clay left, we arranged to meet at the Holiday Inn bar later that night. "Wanna spend the night at my apartment?" he'd asked. When I kissed him back, he knew my answer. With spacious accommodations, good friends as roommates, and a boyfriend who I'd planned to remember as The One, this year was going to be memorable.

"How did you convince your daddy to let you drive from Canton, Ohio, to Greensboro, North Carolina, alone?" Francine asked.

"Now that my dad dates, he's morphed into a more reasonable, less dictatoresque father."

Squaring the sheet corners on my bottom bunk, an irony struck me. Before Mom bolted, she'd been a stickler about clean sheets and well-made bed linens. In the vast menu of PU—parental unit—idiosyncrasies, her neurotic fussiness had been ingrained in me. I couldn't believe that it had been a whole year since my life went schizoid. I know this happens to a lot of families and nowadays is even considered normal-ish. There was nothing normal about my mom leaving us. Without driving down Nitty Gritty Lane, she had skipped out on my dad with her psychic girlfriend in search of her vortex of happy. Since she'd taken flight on her inner-self adventure, Dad started dying his hair, taking step-aerobics classes, and dating the instructor. His girlfriend, Trudy Bleaux, had a personality that residing somewhere between Flake City and Tacky Town. To be fair, she has had one positive effect on him: he'd loosened up on the rules and regulations. Funny how an emotional snowball disturbance can have a benefit.

Jet bunked above Katie Lee, and by default I'd be bunking below Francine. The nut-and-bolt enthusiast kept her jewelry and personal beauty items in a metal container that looked like a fishing tackle box, complete with rusted clasps. It was open on her bed, and she busied herself arranging packages of liquid eyeliner and stud earrings in various compartments. With arms in a wing position, she rocked her behind on the bed. "Y'all, this bunk feels jiggly."

"Top bunks are like that," I said.

Digging in her tackle box, she removed a wrench and jumped down.

"Did you tell the FBI about your Bubba sighting in Canton?" Katie Lee asked.

Swiveling her head, Jet fixed a stare at me. "Whoa. Why would you tell the FBI about someone called Bubba?"

I palmed some wrinkles off my van Gogh *Starry Night* comforter. When I looked up, Jet hadn't dropped the curious gaze she held on me. Her inquisitive manner chimed a warning bell. In a small voice, I said, "Bubba's a wanted man. I called Agent Cauldwell yesterday."

A few hours ago, I'd been making out with Clay and felt guilty at the mention of Bubba. I didn't know Jet from a hole in the wall and didn't want to divulge my deranged tale that I'd had one too many encounters with a guy who's on the FBI wanted list. Determined to ax the drama karma, I lied. "Summer is barely a memory. There's nothing to tell, really."

Jet cranked a wrench counterclockwise on a corner bolt that secured the top bunk to the bottom.

"What are you doing?" I asked.

"They're stripped. I'm gonna replace them."

Nested in her butterfly chair, Francine nibbled the edges of a packaged cherry pie she'd bought from the hallway vending machine. "Bubba Jackson's from New Bern," she said before licking the filling that had dripped onto her wrist.

Jet asked Katie Lee, "Your hometown?"

Before Katie Lee responded, Francine grumbled, "Um-hmm."

In a huff, Katie Lee stepped out of the closet where she'd jammed a season's worth of clothes, shoes, and spare bedding. She put a bulging Gucci wallet with navy Gs printed on it into a matching purse. "Jesus Christ, Francine. You're acting as if New Bern is a cesspool of criminal activity."

"You said it, not me. And watch the JC references. The last thing we need is some bad juju channeling us."

"Francine Battle, I take offense to that comment. Y'all, last year was a total fluke. Normally The Bern is a sleepy Carolina town where nothing ever happens."

"Y'all are killin' me here," Jet said as she loosened another bolt.

"Do you know what you're doing?" I asked.

"I know how to replace a few fasteners," she muttered. "So what happened?"

"Nothing," I said in an attempt to diffuse the electricity that sparked between Katie Lee and Francine.

Pausing to look down her nose at Katie Lee, Francine continued. "Spring semester, Rachael uncovered an art thug. Billy Ray ran his art forgery business out of New Bern and sold 'em across the Southeast. Over Easter break, he cornered her in a bathroom. Like a chicken on an assembly line at a nugget processing plant, he tried to wring her neck. Saved herself by ramming his towel rod."

"I didn't ram his towel rod. I rammed him in the ear with a towel rod."

Francine flicked her wrist. Moving out of her chair, she closed in on Jet. "The thug had a partner called Bubba Jackson—another New Bernian."

Katie Lee snapped, "Don't forget his cousin in Louisiana."

Pulling a large bolt from the bed frame, Jet summoned Francine. "Help me out and hold the bunk for a second."

"Anyone want a soda?" I asked.

Steadying the bed, Francine had the focus of a bird dog flushing a pheasant from scrub. "What are you implyin' about my home state? That man was no local. Just an implant."

"Face it, Francine, New Orleans is a world famous den of depravity. Rach almost got killed down there, too."

"Stop bein' cooyon," Francine said. "It's not the location that almost killed her, it's her choice in company. When you're around, Rachael gets into trouble."

Katie Lee launched her purse. "I will not be spendin' the year with you flinging Cajun insults."

Covering her head with her arms, Francine ducked. Without any support, the top bunk tipped, and Jet's tackle box and its contents splayed to the ground. Jet jumped backward and knocked into Francine, tumbling them both to the floor.

Pointing her index finger at Francine, Katie Lee hissed, "You take that back."

From the floor, Francine shouted, "You can't take back the truth."

Realizing the altercation wasn't going to end without intervention, I placed myself between them.

A knuckle knocked our door and pushed it open. I heard a familiar boot-clank shuffle across the linoleum. The man-with-a-plan for anything female had come calling. Hugh Bass, the guy who'd surreptitiously slept with two of my girlfriends at the same time, without either knowing of the other until the end of freshman year, dared to visit.

Hugh had moves like a frisky kitten, and without warning, he pounced. Wrapped in his arms, Katie Lee and I were bulldozed down. "Miss me?" he asked.

"Damn it, Hugh," Katie Lee shouted.

"Lord Almighty," Francine sang. "That cursin' has attracted the devil's helper."

"Is that any way to greet me after a long summer apart?"

Even though she was down, Francine side-kicked his ass. "Listen here, your head ain't on right."

"Hugh," I squeaked from below. "I'm drowning in armpit."

He made a meal of untwisting himself from the pile, and his hand squeezed my behind before he got to his feet. From above he tugged Francine to her feet. Quick as a lizard tail, she grabbed a toss pillow off of a lower bunk and walloped his head, repeatedly.

"Hey, hey now," he said. "What's that for?"

Francine moved toward a closet mirror. "You don't got the sense God gave a gnat."

Katie Lee sat upright, and he reached his open arms toward her, but reeled when she said, "Some nerve you've got showing up!"

"I was in the area and thought I'd stop by. Invite my favorite girls to celebrate our one-year anniversary."

"What are you talking about?" Katie Lee asked.

"The Holiday Inn. I thought we'd all go over to toast sophomore year."

Not easily spurned, he assessed Jet. Stroking the smooth skin above his lip, he cleared his throat and, in a come-hither drawl, said, "I don't believe I've had the pleasure."

"Jet," she said, and asked, "Can you hold the bunk up so I can screw it?"

"I can help you with that," he said.

Once on my feet, I moved to his ear. "So good to see you. Grab my ass again, or sleep with any more of my roommates, and I'll make sure you think a bag of cold peas down the front of your pants is a good idea."

"Good to see you too, darlin'," he said.

"How's Sheila? Are you two still a thing?" I asked.

Contorting his facial muscles, he answered with a shake of his head. Once he and Jet secured the bunk, he slid a hand inside his jacket and retrieved a small postage-wrapped package.

"What's that?" I asked.

Hugh wiggled his eyebrows. "This year, Grogan's gotten all strict about who comes and goes. When I signed in, the sergeant at the front desk asked if I'd bring it on up to you."

His bait-and-switch tactic worked. I dropped the Sheila-She-Devil topic and focused on the return postage address. Canton, Ohio. Dad had given me the Ford Galaxie and cash from the sale of a painting I'd refurbished. We were in a recession, and business at the shop was slow. I'd seen the books, and profits were slim. I couldn't imagine that he'd send anything else.

"Did Clay-boo send somethin'?" Francine purred.

"Open it," Katie Lee said.

I shook the package. It didn't rattle. "Clay's never been to Ohio."

Moving to my desk, I pulled out a pair of scissors and removed the outer package wrap. It was a black box, and inside rested a hinged purple velvet case and a sealed note.

"Looks expensive," Jet said.

After draping his ass on a corner of my desk, Hugh added commentary. "Rachael is a treasure hunter."

"That's an exaggeration."

Katie Lee dined on argument opportunities and said, "You do have a knack for uncovering things."

I ignored her.

"Before you open that, make sure it isn't cursed or booby-trapped."

Francine had a point. For just-in-cases, before prying the box open, I thumbed the eye of Horus trinket around my neck. A voodoo maven and descendent of Marie Laveau had given it to me, and I'd made a habit of wearing it for luck.

"Well, I'll be damned," Katie Lee said.

"Ain't that sparkly?" Francine quipped.

"What the hell is that glob of gold supposed to be?" Hugh asked.

Jet moved closer, and her eyes widened when she looked at the jeweled oyster brooch I held. "*Crassostrea Virginica*," she said.

"Virgin what?" Hugh asked.

I glared at Katie Lee. *Had she told him about my inexperience?*

Jet elaborated on her brainiac Latin, "A bivalve mollusk."

"What?" I asked.

"An oyster," she said.

As I rotated it in my palm, the fastener triggered a memory. A few years ago I'd watched Edmond, my dad's assistant at the restoration shop, solder a similar fastener when he repaired a vintage tie clip. It was called a trombone clasp since the pin slipped into a barrel, securing the hinge.

Jet piped in, "I was born and raised on brine. My family owns the oldest South Carolina oyster harvestin' plant still in operation. We pull 'em outta the May River." Lowering her voice, she spoke out of the corner of her mouth. "Where I come from, you aren't a real woman until you've eaten a naked half dozen."

With his nimble fingers, Hugh began to unbutton his cotton plaid shirt. "I'll get naked with a half dozen."

"Hugh!" Katie Lee and I rebuked.

Francine pushed past Hugh to make her way to my desk. "That oyster's been gilded and bejeweled. Look at the big purple gem set toward the bottom. Someone besides Clay must have ideas about your libido?"

I studied the artful intricacies of the shell. "If an oyster brooch is bringing thoughts of libido to your mind, maybe you need to focus on your own womanness."

Plucking the sealed card from under the wrapping, Katie Lee handed it to me. "Open the note."

The envelope was weighty, like a wedding invitation. My name had been penned in a decorative loopy script that resembled calligraphy. Sliding my finger to break the wax seal, I noticed the Crane & Co stamp on the bottom. The flat note card had a raspberry-colored border that matched the wax seal.

Darling Rachael,

Seeing you are a sophomore, I wanted you to have something special. An old acquaintance willed this brooch to me, and since you're attending university near the coast, I thought it appropriate to gift the oyster to you.

All the best in your school year. Don't study too much, be sure and have some fun!

Love,

GG

Katie Lee dipped her head over my shoulder. "GG? Who's GG?"

"Grandma Geneva."

"Wait a minute," Francine said. "You told me your grandparents were deceased."

"My dad's mom incarnated over the summer."

"Rewind," Katie Lee said.

Hugh's eyebrows almost connected, Jet's mouth hung open, and Francine twisted her bottom lip under the top.

"Never mind," I said.

Made in the USA
Columbia, SC
28 March 2018